Winning
With Index
Mutual Funds

WINNING WITH INDEX MUTUAL FUNDS

How to Beat Wall Street at Its Own Game

Jerry Tweddell
and
Jack Pierce

American Management Association

New York • Atlanta • Boston • Chicago • Kansas City • San Francisco • Washington, D.C.
Brussels • Mexico City • Tokyo • Toronto

This book is available at a special
discount when ordered in bulk quantities.
For information, contact Special Sales Department,
AMACOM, a division of American Management Association,
1601 Broadway, New York, NY 10019.

This publication is designed to provide accurate and authoritative
information in regard to the subject matter covered. It is sold with the
understanding that the publisher is not engaged in rendering legal,
accounting, or other professional service. If legal advice or other expert
assistance is required, the services of a competent professional person
should be sought.

Library of Congress Cataloging-in-Publication Data
Tweddell, Jerry.
    Winning with index mutual funds : how to beat Wall Street at its
own game / Jerry Tweddell and Jack Pierce.
      p.   cm.
    Includes bibliographical references and index.
    ISBN 0-8144-0358-1
    1. Mutual funds. I. Pierce, Jack. II. Title.
HG4530.T94   1997
332.63´27—dc21   96-47777
                                                        CIP

© 1997 Jerry Tweddell and Jack Pierce.
All rights reserved.
Printed in the United States of America.

This publication may not be reproduced,
stored in a retrieval system,
or transmitted in whole or in part,
in any form or by any means, electronic,
mechanical, photocopying, recording, or otherwise,
without the prior written permission of AMACOM,
a division of American Management Association,
1601 Broadway, New York, NY 10019.

Printing number

10 9 8 7 6 5 4 3 2

To our wives,
Deb Tweddell and **Avril Pierce,**
for their patience, understanding,
and support

Contents

Preface

Very few people can afford to be poor.

George Bernard Shaw

Even after one of the most spectacular bull markets in history, the average mutual fund investor hasn't done nearly as well as the stock market. One reason is that many are still playing by old rules established by Wall Street decades ago. The other stems from the fact that investors have great difficulty overcoming obstacles to success—both real and imagined—that are largely of their own making.

Wall Street's stock in trade is the presumption that the pros know best how you should invest your money. Traditional "full-service" brokers aren't about to disabuse you of this notion—it is immensely profitable. The enormous success of no-load funds and discount brokers has proven that you no longer have to play by the old rules. You don't have to fight the system; you can simply avoid it.

If you have been investing "the old-fashioned way," you've been spending too much money on Wall Street expertise and not investing enough in the market. The phenomenal growth in the number of investors who have kicked the expensive "full-service" broker habit is one of the success stories of the last decade. The weight of the evidence has shown that experts promise and cost far more than they deliver. Enter index funds. Beginning their third decade, they have shown that they also pro-vide higher returns at lower cost.

An index mutual fund is a securities portfolio that seeks to duplicate the return of its target index (such as the Standard & Poor's 500 Index). Most funds try to beat the index. While an index is a mathematical calculation, an index fund holds the actual securities in the same propor-tion as the index.

Understandably, the establishment has been largely silent on the subject because the closer their retail cus-tomers get to indexing, the closer many Wall Streeters are to obsolescence. Even without the help of the pros, many investors have discovered index funds. Vanguard Index Trust 500 Portfolio, the largest and oldest index fund in the country, is enjoying an influx of money that will swell its assets and make them surpass Magellan's—the largest fund—by the turn of the century. But the ranks of investors who understand the benefits of indexing are still remark-ably small. Only 5% of individual investors' mutual fund assets are committed to index funds, compared to one-third of the combined assets of all corporate and public em-ployee pension funds—$350 billion.

The vast majority of mutual fund investors still don't know the index fund "story." Enter *Winning With Index Mu-tual Funds.* This book shows how to use index funds to overcome the five most common obstacles that have de-feated investors for decades:

1. *Investors put their money in the wrong place at the wrong time.* Whether the "place" is stocks, real es-tate, gold, bonds, speculative mutual funds, or baseball cards, they invest too late.
2. *Investors are investment illiterate.* Lacking a basic un-derstanding of investing because they think it is too complicated, they turn to "experts."
3. *Investors allow too much of their money to be siphoned off in fees.* Mutual fund shareholders are paying over

$20 billion a year to have their funds managed and billions more to investment professionals to pick their funds for them. Since most mutual funds trail the major indexes significantly, most of the billions paid for professional management are wasted on demonstrably inferior results.

4. *Investors are too dependent on Wall Street professionals,* who serve themselves and their institutional customers first and their retail customers last.

5. *Investors don't know how to handle risk.* The obsession with risk prevents many from investing during their entire lifetime. History shows that the collective preoccupation with risk soars after a big market drop and virtually disappears during a booming market—inflicting systematic ruin on participants.

In addition to enabling investors to overcome these obstacles, index funds are simple. You don't have to become a financial expert (giving up your Saturday afternoons) because indexing imposes a wonderfully simple and investor-friendly discipline. It allows you to ignore most of Wall Street's static, which only complicates investing and provides little value. Indexing allows you to concentrate on the issues most critical to your success: where to put your money and how to manage risk.

Index funds are not just the latest "product" in the long Wall Street merchandising pipeline, nor are they a gimmick or obscure methodology confined to academia or the fringes of the investment world. Over 150 publicly held index funds have been launched, attracting assets of over $50 billion.

This book provides specific solutions:

Obstacle 1: *Investors put their money in the wrong place at the wrong time.*

Solution:

Obstacle 2: *Investors are investment illiterate.*

Solution:

Obstacle 3: *Investors allow too much of their money to be siphoned off in fees.*

Solution:

Obstacle 4: *Investors are too dependent on Wall Street professionals.*

Solution:

Obstacle 5: *Investors don't know how to handle risk.*

Solution:

Chapter 5   You Bet Your Assets
            Pothole Investing

Most importantly, you learn how, with little time and effort, to significantly improve your mutual fund returns.

Note: For those who are unfamiliar with mutual funds and how they work, read Appendix B, "What You Might Already Know About Mutual Funds." It gives you all the basic information you need to understand the rest of this book.

Acknowledgments

In doing research for this book, we discovered many new developments and options in the evolving index fund field, which made the case for indexing even stronger than we first surmised.

Joan Getsinger and Lorelei Williams provided valuable research assistance, and they remained cheerful even when asked to go out of their way to perform tedious and thankless tasks. For encouragement and enthusiasm all through our project, Shelley Bouhaja was inspirational. For technical assistance, we could not have done without significant help from people who dragged us out of the ice age and unraveled the mysteries of computers, software, and disks. We want to thank Lisa Hyndman, who expertly prepared the charts and graphs and exhibited infinite patience with the endless stream of revisions. We are indebted to Jackie Pierce, who spent very long deadline-beating days developing the format for the entire manuscript and who accomplished more in a short time than we thought possible. Without Gavin Pierce, who provided a state-of-the-art computer and invaluable technical advice, we would never have been able to meet our deadline.

From the start, our agent, Laurie Harper, owner of the Sebastian Literary Agency in San Francisco, promised more than we thought possible—and delivered every time. As the book took form, she contributed valuable encouragement and, as we encountered seemingly insurmountable glitches, she guided us through each one with extraordinary skill and patience. Her best advice: "First of all, don't panic."

Jerry Tweddell

Jack Pierce

1

The First Step: Stop Paying for Bad Advice

It ain't braggin' if you really done it.

Dizzy Dean

Most of us believe that a do-it-yourselfer is an amateur and that, to get the job done properly, you hire a professional. Most of the time, this common wisdom serves us well. If we undertake a project on our own, it is usually to save money, not because we expect a better result.

Take the family car, for example. We approach do-it-yourself tasks with varying levels of skill and enthusiasm—or dread. We might replace the windshield wiper blades, but we don't even think about tearing the engine apart to see what's bothering the camshaft. We just make an appointment with Mr. Goodwrench, deliver the car, and wait for the bad news because, even if we're interested in automechanics, we don't have the skills, the equipment, or the time to attempt the repairs.

Experts *usually* make things better: Your car's performance improves and it will likely last longer. Why should hiring a mutual fund expert be any different? To the uninitiated, yield to maturities and portfolio turnover rates are just as alien as valve lifters and piston rings. Even if you have a vague idea of what they are, you are clueless as to what to do about them. Once again, it seems like a good time to bring in the experts.

Or is it? As backward as it may seem, most of the experts you hire to work on your mutual funds only make things worse. Statistics show that the benefits (the returns) that experts provide don't make up for what they cost (in management fees and sales charges).

The difference is that owning mutual fund shares doesn't have to be like owning the family car. Your car can't maintain itself, and you're stuck with the costs of keeping it running. But you can get around costly mutual fund maintenance expenses with index funds—because they maintain themselves. Once you buy a car and drive it off the lot, how much you paid over dealer's cost has no bearing on how well it runs. It's no different with mutual funds; no-load investors have already figured that out.

Yet investors are reluctant to attempt do-it-yourself investing because they view it as too "serious" an undertaking. Brokers spend millions of advertising dollars encouraging that very notion: Investors are portrayed as helplessly adrift on stormy seas, desperately in need of an expert and experienced hand at the helm—which only Wall Street can provide.

While a great many no-load investors have found that they no longer need someone to choose funds for them, most still feel that they need somebody to manage them. Fund investors still have 95% of their money managed by pros. But do they have to? Paradoxically, for most of their mutual fund money, the answer is an unqualified no. A small and fast-growing minority has discovered that they are better off *without* professional management, and the number of do-it-yourself investors is growing. Over 20 years of results, since the first index fund appeared in 1976, haven't proven them wrong.

Do-it-yourself index fund returns don't beat all the pros every year, but they outperform them most of the time. That consistency, year after year, mounts up with impressive results, and the vast majority of professional fund managers would be delighted to have done as well as the amateurs have done in the past two decades.

The Investment Illiterates: The Little Fish

If you don't know where you're going, you'll end up somewhere else.

Yogi Berra

Normally indefatigable do-it-yourselfers, Americans are largely investment illiterate and seemingly not too concerned about it. While they might work hard at their jobs, they appear to be somewhat indifferent to investing their money. As a result, most Americans are underinvested, badly invested, or not invested at all.

Why? One good reason is that U.S. tax rates on investment returns are among the highest in the industrialized world. Another is the belief that investing is simply too complicated. Still another is the perception that "the big boys" have somehow stacked the odds against "the little guy," a notion that in some cases is uncomfortably close to the truth. Another reason is cultural; some Americans feel that investing is for the greedy. Even those who feel its necessity often prefer to delegate the unpleasant task to others. Little credit is given to investors who take responsibility for their own destiny and who, when successful, are unlikely to become burdens on society.

Reinforcing the cultural indifference to investing is the U.S. public education system, which ignores investing as a worthy subject, except for the occasional high school guest speaker or community college evening course. If proper emphasis were placed on investing in our high schools and colleges, students would learn the enormous importance—and simplicity—of compounding equity versus savings returns. As shown by the Compound Growth table in Appendix D, over 35 years every dollar invested at a typical savings rate of 5% grows over five-fold. At stocks' historic 10% returns, it grows over 28 times!

Ignorant of investing basics, students are urged by their valedictorians to go forth and be successful. Banks then convince them that they are investing when they are saving, and brokers talk them into buying speculative merchandise when they should be investing. And, because far too many don't know what realistic investment returns are, investors continue to be defrauded out of millions of dollars by scheme operators promising ludicrously high returns. The common denominator is investment illiteracy.

Investment illiteracy is not confined to the blue-collar world. It is not uncommon for highly educated, otherwise financially successful people to be investment illiterate. A survey taken by The Consumer Federation and The American Association of Retired Persons found that 82% of consumers whose banks sell mutual funds believed that those funds were insured against loss—or simply didn't know whether they were insured or not. Even the Federal Reserve System is concerned; they included the fact that mutual funds aren't guaranteed or insured in a recent video, *Mutual Funds: Understanding the Risks.*

An even more disheartening survey by *Money* found that 47% of those surveyed believed that, if they invested in stock or stock market funds, "they would lose 100% of their investment at some time in their lives." These statistics show a remarkable lack of understanding of even the most basic investment principles; it is small wonder that so many Americans just "leave it in the bank."

Wall Street's merchandising techniques don't help. If you happen to live in the right neighborhood, you are probably plagued with irritating dinnertime phone calls from obnoxious script-reading cold callers. It hardly makes the investment process appealing; many approach it with the same dread as buying a car.

Also, all too often, taking the Wall Street plunge ends up badly. Because few investors have realistic reference points, they invest in shoddy merchandise that primarily benefits brokers and institutions instead of themselves. Making this volatile mixture even more dangerous is investors' proclivity, knowing that they have "missed" a major part of the up cycle—to naively think they can catch up. Too often, the tendency is to forsake conservative, quality investments in favor of aggressive and risky products. Making matters worse, they are also likely to pay too much in fees. This costly and belated rush to "get in on a good thing" usually turns out with predictably poor results.

Are You Really in Good Hands?

Without understanding the rudimentary principles of investing, most individuals place their faith in expert professionals.

That faith is usually misplaced. How else can you explain the fact that most people continue to invest in funds that deliver below-average returns year after year? This odd detachment is costing them hundreds of billions of dollars a year in subpar returns and wasted fees.

One explanation is that, after handing over investment responsibilities to someone else, few measure their results, know how to measure them, or know what to measure them against. If results are mediocre or poor, fewer still have any idea about how to improve them. If results are really awful, the investor usually replaces one set of professionals with another, often only making things worse.

A further explanation is that investing is perceived as a complicated and demanding activity: To be successful, you must become totally immersed. Short of that, common wisdom is to hire an investment pro—of whom there is no shortage. To more than half a million brokers and 600 mutual fund management companies running over 8,000 mutual funds, add financial planners, insurance salespeople, and financial advisors.

An odd kind of problem is that it's hard to tell the real experts in this enormous population of professionals because everyone is prospering from one of history's longest-running bull markets. With the financial services industry enjoying unprecedented prosperity, most professionals are enjoying record profits regardless of their ability.

Possibly due in part to the "camouflage" of overall prosperity, Americans, if you judge them by their investment buying patterns, are either satisfied with the results or don't know what to do to get their money's worth. More than ever, Americans are turning to fund managers to solve their investment dilemmas. Fifteen years ago, before one of the biggest bull markets ever, only one in 16 Americans was a fund investor. Today, after 15 years of historically above-average returns, it is one in four, and total mutual fund assets have grown from $50 billion in 1980 to over $3 trillion. Today, the giant Magellan Fund alone has more assets than were held by all equity mutual funds at the beginning of the 1980s.

From their inception in 1924, equity mutual funds have always suffered from bear markets, when prices fall and shareholders depart, and fared spectacularly when the bulls were in charge. The extended 1980s through 1990s bull market is no exception. Over 70% of the money invested in U.S. stock funds has been invested since 1991 and *more money poured into equity mutual funds during the first four months of 1996 than was invested during the first forty years of their existence.*

So the investment illiterates—the little fish—swim in the same waters as the money movers—the big fish.

The Money Movers: The Big Fish

If you mean to profit, learn to please.

Winston Churchill

"Merrill will spend $130 million on world-wide research this year, helping clients save money by knowing exactly when to buy or sell their stocks," John L. Steffins, Broker-age Chief of Merrill Lynch told *The Wall Street Journal* in 1994. The startling disclosure that Merrill Lynch has solved the most bedeviling of investment problems went largely unnoticed by the press. And to think that knowing exactly when to buy and sell stocks has just plumb evaded us all this time. Although Merrill has solved the biggest of investors' problems, a few remain. You should know not only what brokers do *for* you, but also what they can do *to* you.

You're a Consumer, Not a Client

While investment results are your primary interest, they are only a distant concern of brokerage firm management. Customers may look to stockbrokers as advisors, but brokerage managers view them primarily as salespeople and distributors. This is a significant problem because the two concerns are basically incompatible. The more success the house has in extracting fees and commissions from customers' accounts, the less there is left to invest; this, of course, proportionately diminishes the chances of superior returns.

So brokers are not paid to manage money: They are salespeople who receive commissions when they *move money.* How much, how often, and where they move it all determine the size of their next commission check. The industry has tried to develop more income from fees, but money moving remains the main source of most brokers' incomes. As in any business, no broker is completely immune to a touch of avarice and/or management pressure. No doubt many suitable and excellent investments are recommended. There is also no doubt that, at times, even the most conscientious broker is faced with helping to distribute questionable or even awful packaged products or syndicate offerings because of the high mark-up. Transactions are the source of income for brokers. All else being equal, brokers are just as likely to discourage trading as your barber is to tell you you don't need a haircut.

All That Money Wall Street Spends on Research— Wasted ...

The stock market had been drifting in the summer doldrums for weeks. Customers who weren't on vacation had little interest in the market and commissions were way down. Our frustrated branch manager called us into the conference room for yet another sales meeting. When the wise-cracking died down, he picked up a telephone and swept it over the assembled brokers. "This, ladies and gentlemen, is a telephone. Your job is to pick it up and call people. Your job is then to find out what the (bleep) they want to buy. And then, (bleep) it," he bellowed, "your (bleeping) job is to SELL IT to them!" So much for good old-fashioned Wall Street research ....

Another problem is that customers usually have to be sold on each investment. Few salespeople survive, let alone prosper, offering "only" average or below-average results. Brokers *have to* predict superior results. This is no small problem: The law of averages does not allow all 500,000, or even most, brokers to deliver such results; it is mathematically impossible. Since most investors' after-costs results turn out below average, most of them are disappointed.

This brings up still another irony. Full-service brokers are the highest-cost providers of financial services. Compared to most other providers, their customers have the least left over to invest after costs. They are therefore the least likely to get above-average results.

If that weren't enough, decades-old conflicts of interest are embedded in the full-service brokerage industry. In addition to retail customers, these brokers serve institutions such as banks, insurance companies, mutual funds, and investment banking customers (corporations that issue stocks and bonds). When conflicting interests converge, retail customers usually find themselves at the bottom of the totem pole.

It's All in the Packaging

Volumes have been written on the failed oil, gas, and real estate partnerships of the 1980s, on the "enhanced" income mutual funds that promised more but delivered less income, on the annuities that collapsed, etc.—all packages brought to you by brokers. The further you go back in the history books, the longer the sorry list gets. Major brokerage firms are still negotiating settlements with the SEC and former investors in imploded limited partnerships, and their still-climbing tab is over $2.5 billion.

For a recent example, look back no further than the proliferation of almost sure-fire losers—closed-end fund initial public offerings (IPOs). In 1994, $7.9 billion worth of them were sold to the public, and, even though the S&P rose slightly that year, 37 of 39 (95%) of these offerings were losers. (More about these products a little later in this chapter.)

Common threads run through such customer-buster packaged products:

* They are created and packaged by institutions and/or corporations on a wholesale basis, and they are distributed to retail customers by brokers who charge more than the usual retail commissions.
* They promise something "extra"—higher returns—that supposedly only professionals provide.
* They are the current rage on Wall Street, and institutions create them at a heady clip to meet demand.
* They deliver below-average returns to most retail customers—and way below-average to many more investors.

The IPO "PU"—A Case Study in Customer Busting

Promoters are just guys with two pieces of bread looking for
a piece of cheese.

Evel Knievel

An activity that is hugely profitable for brokers and fraught with peril for retail customers is the initial public offering (IPO). *Forbes* magazine reported a study of returns of 4,753 new issues over the 1970 through 1990 period; their conclusion: "New issues stink." Five-year returns were almost 60% less than "a statistically matched sample of companies that weren't newly public." The purchase prices used in the study were from the day after the IPO. They have be the "day-old" prices because, if you have ever tried to buy an IPO that was in demand (a "hot deal"), you know that it is virtually impossible. Institutions get served first.

Even if you are fortunate enough to get a few token shares, a retail customer playing the "syndicate calendar" on a continual basis is a financial masochist. The only offerings available in meaningful amounts are those that institutions don't want. If you can get all you want of an IPO, the odds are overwhelming that you don't want it. For retail investors, the syndicate calendar is a stacked game whose primary rule is something like "heads you win a little, tails you lose a lot."

The Greatest Stink of All: The Closed-End Fund IPO

One of the many reasons "broker bashing" has come into vogue is the brokerage industry's long-standing practice of distributing *closed-end fund* IPOs to their retail customers. If this doesn't make you think that a few more bashes are in order, probably nothing will.

If you have been dealing with a full-service broker, you have probably been encouraged at one time or another to invest in a closed-end fund IPO because, until very recently, Wall Street has distributed them by the tens of billions of dollars every year.

It's a nifty arrangement for brokers. The commission is two or three times the posted rates, and there is a deadline for customers to get "in" on the offering. This "time close" allows brokers to pressure customers for a decision rather than hearing that most-hated customer response: "I'm going to think about it for a while." And, because the trade confirmation doesn't show the commission, some unscrupulous brokers aren't beyond telling naive customers that the fund—not the investor—pays the commission.

It's the Commission, Stupid.

The reason that brokers distribute closed-end funds to their customers is easy to understand when you look at how they get paid. *Money* magazine (June 1992) calculated "how much an average broker would make on nine different $10,000 transactions":

Closed-end fund (new offering)	$247
Mutual fund (open end)	238
Limited partnership	233
Unit investment trust (new offering)	171
Common stock (new offering)	171
Closed-end fund (secondary market)	86
Common stock	86
Corporate bond (long-term)	76
U.S. Treasury bond, note, bill	19

At their zenith in the late 1920s, there were about 400 closed-end trusts—forerunners of today's closed-end funds—worth about $4.5 billion. Largely because they were highly leveraged, only a half-dozen survived the 1929 crash and are still in existence today. For decades, they were forgotten fund orphans; during the late 1960s and 1970s, less than $3.0 billion worth were launched.

Interest began to return in the 1980s, and by the 1990s the trickle grew into a flood. In the years 1992 through 1994, Wall Street distributed 273 funds worth $44.2 billion garnering approximately $3.0 billion in commissions.

While these IPOs made brokers significantly wealthier, they had the opposite effect on their retail customers. In 1994, a year when the S&P 500 rose slightly, the price on the average closed-end fund was down 13%, and, as already mentioned, of the 39 closed-end fund IPOs launched that year, 37 lost money for their investors.

There are two simple rules to closed-end fund investing:

* Never invest at net asset value (NAV).
* Never, never invest at a premium to NAV.

The reason is painfully simple: *Closed-end funds sell at discounts most of the time.* At the end of 1993, 63% of almost 500 closed-ends were selling at discounts; by August 1995, the percentage had increased to 84%.

Discounts tend to widen during bear markets, and they narrow when investors are optimistic and prices are rising. Discounts of 10 to 15% are usual. The Herzfeld Closed-Fund Average, which tracks the discounts of 17 equity funds, was recently at 13%.

With discounts widening and narrowing subject to the whims of public psychology, the discount introduces a variable—the very opposite of what you want to do in the investing process. Bearish sentiment drove prices of some funds to 50% discounts in 1974, and the risk that it might happen again eliminates our recommending closed-ends at today's "normal" discounts. The risk/reward is particularly lousy because premiums do not occur often, and they are not very large when they do (10% or more is rare indeed). So buying a closed-end fund at an abnormal premium in a world where discounts are normal is obviously a monumentally bad idea, coming close to a sure-fire way to lose money.

But that is exactly what a closed-end fund IPO is: a customer-buster. Exhibit 1-1 shows a typical offering distributed to retail investors (institutions, who know better, avoid them) at $10 per share, which then drops on the open market to a business-as-usual discount. Year after year, brokers have routinely distributed billions of dollars worth of these "automatic" losses to their customers, apparently without even a twinge of the collective Wall Street conscience.

A textbook example of a closed-end fund IPO gone south-and-sour was the 20-million-share offering of Global Health Sciences distributed to retail investors January 16, 1992 at $15 per share.

The fund was to be managed by the very well regarded John Kaweske, who had been running the extremely successful no-load open-end Financial Health Sciences Portfolio fund for the previous five years. Under Kaweske's stewardship, according to the prospectus, his fund "ranked #1 out of all the 1,347 registered open-end investment companies ranked by Lipper." It had compounded at a remarkable 33.3% annual rate the previous five years and 92.9% in the 12 months prior to the offering.

Global Health Sciences was a typical closed-end IPO with one notable exception: The no-load it was cloned from remained open and was still available. This posed an obvi-

Exhibit 1-1. Customer-buster arithmetic.

Closed-End Fund IPO Purchased at $10 Per Share

$10.00	Offering price
.70	Commission
9.30	NAV remaining

The Business-as-Usual Discount

	8.37	10% discount	**16.3% loss**
Recent Average:	8.09	13% discount	**19.1% loss**
	7.44	20% discount	**25.6% loss**

ous question: Why would investors pay an admission price when they could get in for free? The delicate situation was neatly solved by making the "new" fund just different enough to be "different." Then again, it wasn't all that different; after all, why would anyone want to be too different from the "#1" fund in the country?

In one day, egged on by exuberant brokers, retail investors plowed in $345 million—more money than had been invested in the no-load sister fund during its entire seven-year life. The distributors collected over $24 million in commissions as investors paid $15 for shares with a NAV of $13.95.

Global Health Sciences began trading on the New York Stock Exchange at $15, made a monumental move to $15⅛—then promptly rolled over and headed south. The Clintons trained their guns on health care, and the stock price fell through its declining NAV and finished the year just above $9 per share at a business-as-usual 10%-plus discount. In less than a year, investors lost over $100 million, over a third of their investment and two and a half times the 13.8% loss experienced by the sister no-load fund.

Other than the availability of its no-load clone (run by the same portfolio manager), Global Health Sciences' IPO was no different from the hundreds of closed-end IPOs floated by Wall Street distributors in recent years. Admittedly, the consequences were more swift and dramatic than usual, but the unforgiving customer-busting arithmetic is standard operating procedure.

There were footnotes to this dreary tale: The famed Mr. Kaweske was terminated by fund management for alleged wrongdoings, and his successor departed in 1996 to start his own management firm. Most important: It took over three and a half years for shareholders just to break even, while the S&P 500 index tacked on 25%.

For the time being, closed-end fund IPO distributors appear to have finally worn out their welcome. The ranks of retail customers—those who didn't know better—were so thinned that by 1994 only 43 IPOs came to market, down from 121 the year before. Underwriters managed to limp out with just five during the first six months of 1995. If there were any attempts during the last half of 1995, they weren't successful: None made it.

How soon will they return? Since they are so profitable to brokers and fund sponsors, as soon as underwriters can lasso enough buyers. Successful roundups of IPO buyers will require unpleasant memories to fade, and a new generation of folks who haven't been burned. If distributors can add some mechanisms so that investors don't take such a swift and sure bashing, it could hasten their comeback.

And You Pay for All This "Service"

Look no further than full-service posted commission rates to get an indication of the retail customer's place in the Wall Street food chain. The Justice Department abolished fixed commissions in 1975, despite the industry's howls of protest. Before then, everybody—little fish and Fidelity alike—paid the same commissions to buy and sell stocks. Today, the small investor pays an average of 42 cents a share—a whopping premium compared to the average 6 cents paid by his brokerage firm's institutional customers.

Throughout the increasing publicity about brokerage firms paying for order flow, shenanigans by NASDAQ traders, rogue brokers, increased fees, and charges and shabby mutual fund practices by banks, there is a common thread: They all take another piece out of the retail customer's hide. The continuing exodus of "small investors" to discount brokers and no-load funds is evidence that more and more of them are concluding that, with friends like these, who needs friends?

The growth of no-load funds and discount brokers is hardly surprising. There is no wiggle room in full-service brokers' most basic pitch—to promise more even if they deliver less. Increasingly, investors understand that, while lowering the cost factor in their investment equation guarantees nothing, at least it puts them ahead by the amount saved. And, as the years pass, those savings compound and mount up to a lot more than unfulfilled promises.

Broker Nightmares: Index Funds

Progress might have been all right once, but it has gone on too long.

Ogden Nash

Even though no-load index funds outperform most professionally managed mutual funds, with a few minor exceptions, major Wall Street full-service brokerage firms don't sell them. Until very recently, brokers sold only load funds because that was how they generated sales commissions.

Retail stockbrokers' stock in trade is investment advice and guidance. As advertised, their function is to analyze and select professionally managed funds that are best for their customers. Once invested, customers then look to brokers to monitor and report on the selected funds' performance and to recommend an occasional fine-tuning.

But how valuable is the stockbroker's advice? Brokers contend that one of their most important functions is keeping customers from panicking during bear markets. Is this true or only wishful thinking? According to *Morningstar's* editor, John Rekenthaler (October 1, 1993), history proves it to be false:

> Aside from Spring 1987, when direct-marketed muni-fund investors wrote checks against their accounts during an interest-rate spike, ... load and no-load funds have behaved similarly during market de-

clines…. Indeed, given that many fund objectives that have suffered big redemptions are dominated by load products, one could seriously argue the reverse case.*

What is not widely advertised is that most broker-sold managed funds trail the results of index funds. From the investor's standpoint, this in itself creates substantial doubt as to the value of stockbrokers' advice: Why be restricted in your choice of funds to a universe of average laggard funds?

A far better approach—as more and more investors are realizing—is to consider *all funds*—including no-load and index funds.

The Wannabe Index Funds

Full-service brokers have lost half the mutual fund buyers to no-load competition. Up to now, their strategy has been to reduce and camouflage sales charges with a dizzying array of front-end, back-end, and level loads—plus an alphabet soup of share classes and 12b-1 fees. But the subterfuge has done little to slow the exodus. More and more former load fund customers are heading for the exits, and the defectors are unlikely to return.

A study done by Goldman, Sachs & Co. in 1995 found that no-load funds grew 160% faster than broker-sold load funds did in the previous nine years. The study also polled investors' intentions, and the results indicate an even bleaker future for mutual fund salespeople:

* 41% used full-service brokers to buy their first fund.
* 32% used a full-service broker to make their most recent fund purchase.
* 25% said they planned to use a full-service broker to make their *next* purchase.

*Morningstar Mutual Funds, Morningstar, Inc., Chicago, Illinois, 800-876-5005.

If no-load funds are a better approach, index funds are the best approach in many respects. Low-cost unmanaged index funds might give nightmares, but, if brokers could turn a buck or two, they might consider selling them. But selling index funds creates a problem: Once customers' money has been indexed, the odds are low that it can be lured back into the more costly broker-sold managed funds. While retail customers may be largely investment illiterate, they aren't stupid. Once they're onto something, they are remarkably quick learners.

Full-service brokers have seen the future—and they don't like it. In order to cope, they have cobbled together programs to try to staunch the flow of customer defections. Merrill Lynch's new "Asset Power" program (a new breakfast cereal?), Smith Barney"s TRAK Personalized Investment Advisory Service, Prudential's PruChoice and others like it are offering "no-load fund supermarkets" for the first time.

The catch? Annual fees averaging 1.5%—totaling 15% of the amount invested in only ten years. That's in addition to 2.0% yearly operating costs of the average stock fund. The grand total of 3.5% annual overhead exacted upon fund supermarket investors is so burdensome that the prospect of even *average* returns is remote. Below-average returns will be the norm.

Indexing Is Out of the Closet

Index funds loom as a much less immediate threat to brokers than no-load funds. Few retail investors know much about indexing—and fewer still are interested in them, as evidenced by the fact that only 5% of their $3 trillion mutual fund holdings is in index funds. Until recently, index funds were few in number, and not much information was available about them. Nor was there evidence that indexing worked. With few exceptions, the handful of index funds available was not promoted and had relatively short histories.

But the threat could be much more menacing than that of no-loads. Large pension funds across the country tuned in a long time ago—with over 30% of their assets indexed. The money managers and banks running index funds are probably less than thrilled because profit margins are slim at best. They have no choice but to include indexing to compete in the modern institutional investment world; it is far too big a phenomenon to ignore, and their sophisticated clients demand it.

So index funds are proliferating, and the oldest fund is now 20 years old. Brokers' nightmares nowadays should include index fund results that have been too good to remain in the closet. Journalistically, they haven't been much talked about because indexing is about as glamorous as a box of rocks. How many interesting articles can be written on mechanically driven funds with no personalities or investment concepts?

Particularly disconcerting to forward-thinking brokers is that customers are bound to notice that winning index funds keep showing up in the financial press with annoying regularity, while managed funds move into and out of the winner's circle subject to style and sector-driven cycles of the market. Customers might not understand exactly how things work, but they are quick to pick up on what works. After that, the finding-out-how part is easy.

The destiny of Wall Street's stockbrokers aside, investing your money most effectively is your highest priority. Brokers don't recommend index funds because they don't get paid for selling them. But brokers' sleep will be troubled even more in the future because their customers, already encouraged by their success with no-loads, are getting the drift of index funds.

Indexing is easy to understand. You don't have to be an investment expert. You only have to understand a few basic principles, not all the minutia of the investment world. You can live your whole life investing successfully without ever knowing exactly how a convertible subordinated debenture works. To tell time, you don't have to build a clock.

More importantly, you don't have to pay for an expert to invest successfully in index funds. With a very simple and basic understanding of index funds, you can consistently beat 70 to 80% of all professionally managed mutual funds.

If you're already a fund investor, the odds are very high that, contrary to your expectations, your funds have delivered below-average returns. You have not beaten the market—the market has consistently beaten you.

Improving your results to "just" average and compounding the improvement provides a surprisingly big bonus, and you can be confident that you won't be making a bad situation worse. And, of course, the part of your investment that isn't siphoned off to a broker is just one reason that index funds deliver better returns.

If you're just getting started, indexing gets you off on the right foot immediately without all the false starts that plague so many beginning investors. Time is possibly the most important element in investing. By saving the time that so many others waste on costly trial-and-error investments, you'll be well on your way to success.

2

The Second Step: Eliminate the Costly Alternatives

Stock investors have the choice of owning either individual stocks, mutual funds, or both. For inexperienced investors, mutual funds, although they might not appear as "exciting" as stocks, are particularly suitable—if for no other reason than that they provide the relative safety of instant diversification. If, after some experience, you feel you can do better than the pros and, most importantly, the indexes, then you might consider a stock portfolio. After all, somebody has to get above-average results, and no law says it can't be you. Realize, though, that you are defying the odds and ignoring the basic indexing premise: Over the long term, like Mother Nature, Mother Market is smarter than almost all the folks trying to beat her.

Stocks Versus Stock Mutual Funds

When you come to a fork in the road, take it.

Yogi Berra

We agree with the experts who advise that people with relatively small amounts of money should invest in funds and that an individual stock portfolio could be considered only if a substantial sum is available. A reasonable threshold for a stock portfolio seems to be $50,000. The larger the sum, the more a stock portfolio might make sense.

For the most part, managing a stock portfolio is more than most of us can handle—along with everything else life demands of us. While some investors have the time, interest, background, capital, and discipline to manage an individual portfolio successfully, they are a small minority. How many can boast of growing their portfolio eightfold over the last 15 years or close to fourfold over the last ten years—as Vanguard Index 500 shareholders have done? How many even know how they have been doing? And compared to what? The answer is precious few. Sadly, too many stock investors confuse playing—and enjoying—the game with winning it.

In addition, expecting a lot of help from your broker is just not realistic. Some brokers are experienced and hardworking, and they toil against the odds trying to do the very best for their customers. Unfortunately, they too are in the minority. It is by design that we have not painted a very pretty picture of stock investing at a full-service brokerage firm.

Considering the fact that brokerage firms' sophisticated systems provide vast amounts of computing power, why is that power not applied in reporting their customers' results? While some firms are beginning to provide percentage return information to their retail brokers, year-to-date or twelve-month returns and how they compare to major benchmark indexes or averages—Information Age 101 stuff—is noticeably absent on customers' statements. When it is provided, customers have to request it. It would seem that if most retail customers' returns sparkled, brokers would be eager to trumpet the good news. The logical conclusion: Most of the time, the news ain't good.

For most individual investors, we feel that a mutual fund portfolio has the following advantages:

* Mutual funds offer instant diversification, which lowers your risk. A big drop in a single stock in a 500-stock portfolio doesn't have much effect on your bottom line.

* Mutual funds offer an increasing range of selection. With over 8,000 funds available, there are mutual funds that should meet your requirements, whatever they are.

* Mutual funds are efficient. You can diversify into a wide variety of markets and sectors with limited capital.

* Your investments are professionally managed. Although index funds beat the performance of most professionally managed funds, you can bet your debentures that, over time, most professional managers do better than most novice investors. In addition, professional management can provide added value if you venture into nonmainstream markets, such as small-cap stocks or junk bonds.

* You invest with convenience. Funds are easy to buy and sell, as is switching from one fund to another in a family.

* It's hard to beat the cost-effectiveness of a fund. Even managed funds, with 2% annual operating costs, carry less overhead than most individual stock portfolios. Most brokerage accounts generate commission percentages higher than that. By comparison, an index fund portfolio with annual costs of 0.20 to 0.30% is even more cost-effective.

For most investors, then, mutual funds are the best bet. And for most mutual fund investors, index funds are an even better bet.

However, if you insist on investing in stocks, you can follow certain specific strategies to increase your odds for success (and to keep you from making serious mistakes). Exhibit 2-1 lists our do's and don'ts.

(text continues on page 26)

Exhibit 2-1. The do's and don'ts of investing in stocks.

---

* *Do* index at least half your assets while you are learning the ropes. At a fraction of your costs, institutions have access to virtually any analyst, technician, strategist, economist, or arbitrageur at any brokerage firm in the country. If they, who get the red carpet treatment, index a third of their assets, does it not make sense for you—relegated to the servants' entrance—to do the same? Until you have proven that you are one of the chosen few who can beat the market, index at least one-half of your assets.

* *Don't* confuse brains with a bull market. Don't decide that you are another Peter Lynch or Warren Buffett until you've gone through one complete market cycle—both up and down. Remember: It's not how much you make, it's how much you keep.

* *Don't* confuse winning a few battles with winning the war. Keep score. Before indexing, it wasn't easy to gauge your success. Compare your bottom-line results with the indexes, including all expenses for investment services, magazines, etc. And forget rationalizing, "Oh, I had a great year except for Hapistat Industrial. I won't make that kind of mistake next year." If Hapistat ruined the year's bottom line, admit it. Don't make up excuses.

* *Don't* do business with rookie brokers. Because they have to build a customer base, they are the most likely to spend time and effort soliciting your business. Most have only token investment perspective, and they are under the most intense pressure to generate trades and to push packaged customer-buster products. Three-quarters of them wash out their first year.

* *Do* diversify. One study showed the average brokerage firm account holding only six stocks. To be properly diversified, an account should have at least 20 or 25. David Dreman, a successful money manager, author, and *Forbes* columnist, recommends 25 to 35 issues spread among 16 to 18 industries. In increasingly volatile markets, an "accident"—totally unexpected bad news—that drops a stock 20 to 40% in a few days is not unusual. In a portfolio with only a few issues, it ruins not only your day, but also your portfolio's returns for a year—or maybe more.

* *Do* expect to spend time on your portfolio. For most of us, the scarcest commodity in our lives, besides money, is time. As-

suming that you are properly diversified, you have created a management task for somebody. Even if he or she wanted to, time won't permit even the most conscientious broker with hundreds of clients to watch each of your holdings. The burden falls on you, which may pose a problem.

* *Don't* invest in the packaged products or in the constant stream of syndicate offerings that brokers are under pressure to distribute. Wall Street never stops coming up with "new" products and services, and it is very difficult for even the savviest investor to separate a real investment opportunity from just another customer-buster. Rule of thumb: Let somebody else try them out.

* *Do* have an overall plan. Far too many people have no discipline or overall strategy. Most start out with a plan, but many end up with a collection of miscellaneous stocks, unequally weighted, purchased over the years for various reasons (some forgotten), resulting in a portfolio that flounders with no plan or direction.

* *Don't* get buried by too much information (incredibly plentiful on Wall Street), which diverts you from the critical importance of asset allocation and risk management. Investment success is a function of discipline and simplicity—not of large quantities of information.

* *Don't* put much faith in forecasts and projections. Most stocks are bought on the basis of security analysts' expectations and forecasts of future earnings per share. Almost all written stock recommendations start with a table carrying the analyst's earnings estimates for current and future years; it is usually the heart and soul of the recommendation. Since forecasting is a dicey business, unsurprisingly, most are off the mark—and many are *far* off the mark. *Forbes'* columnist David Dreman (October 10, 1994) has pointed out, "... most investors bet heavily on analysts' forecasts. If they were to study the record, they would realize that missing badly is the rule, not the exception." The latest of a number of studies he has reported was of 66,100 consensus earnings forecasts over the 1974 through 1990 period (a minimum of six analysts per estimate). The conclusion: "Even stacking the deck in favor of the estimates, the average error was 44% annually." To stomach this kind of fare on a continual basis, you need a cast-iron belly.

The Loaded Question: Just Say No

Benjamin Franklin may have discovered electricity, but it was the man who invented the meter who made the money.

Earl Wilson

For those who don't have the time or ability to manage stocks, managed mutual funds seem like the logical choice. Despite all the discouraging facts about full-service brokers, according to the Investment Company Institute, many investors still feel the "need for advice" before investing. For this need, many investors pay the price. The question of whether to pay the sales charge has been talked about often, perhaps more than most people want to hear. Our goal, however, is to encourage you to invest most of your money in index funds—where little or no advice is needed. So we'll say it one more time: In addition to the conflicts of interest and cost considerations, buying load funds from brokers carries other specific and important disadvantages.

Costs

Besides the fact that sales loads don't improve results, in most cases they are much too high for the quality of services rendered. It is not unusual for investors who have just retired to roll over a couple of hundred thousand dollars into an IRA, typically generating commissions of around $8,000 to $10,000. This is a hefty price to pay, particularly if the advice is no more than a warmed-over serving of mediocre in-house funds. Investors so served are paying brain surgeon fees for parking lot attendant services.

But it gets worse! Investors in the new mutual fund wrap programs—where they pay ongoing fees forever—are even worse off: They are paying load-fund equivalent fees and higher to buy no-load funds!

Another unfortunate by-product of sales loads is the fact that the annual expense ratio is higher than for no-load funds. Not only is the price of admission higher, but so are the annual dues. *Morningstar*'s Catherine Voss Sanders (June 23, 1995) calculated just how much higher:*

	No-Load Funds	Load Funds
Expense ratio:	1.11%	1.62%

Not only do most fund investors not realize that higher expense ratios come as part of the sales load package, but as Susan Woodward, the SEC's chief economist observes, "It appears that fundholders don't have a clue how important expenses are (*Money*, February 1995)."

*Morningstar Mutual Funds, Morningstar, Inc., Chicago, Illinois, 800-876-5005.

Restrictions

Although full-service brokers are caving into no-load competition with "no-load" wannabe programs, investors are still restricted to only the funds offered by their broker. Competitors' funds, many no-load funds, and index funds are eliminated from consideration. Just about anywhere but Wall Street, paying extra means an increase rather than a decrease in selection.

Biased Advice

It wasn't too many years ago that brokerage firms had contests—awarding vacation trips, golf clubs, VCRs, and the like to brokers who pushed certain products. Under the glare of publicity, the practice has been largely discontinued, but some banks (who sell about 11% of all load funds), still award contest prizes to their salespeople.

In recent years, publicity and regulatory pressure have forced full-service brokerage firms to end their long-standing practice of paying brokers more to sell their in-house funds. *The Wall Street Journal,* in reporting that one of the last holdouts, Dean Witter, was giving up in late 1995, quoted an observer, "... Having an automaton, a mindless product-purveyor ... doesn't help anyone."

The extra incentives paid to salespeople apparently worked well: Among full-service brokers, total assets in Dean Witter's stock funds trailed only industry giant Merrill Lynch. While Dean Witter may have been very skillful gathering money, they have been less adroit managing it; their stock funds' returns have trailed most competitors. But Dean Witter is not alone in this respect. Most broker-managed funds have been certifiably lousy. *Forbes* magazine, in its annual 1995 mutual fund issue, ranked the 25 largest fund management companies according to returns. No broker-managed fund family shows up in the top five; further, not one even ranked in the top ten. In fact, *the returns of every single broker-managed fund family showed up in the bottom half!*

Most brokerage firms claim they have given up pushing their own funds at the expense of other funds. If so, that doesn't help investors victimized by sales campaigns and incentives in the past resulting in hundreds of billions of dollars languishing in subpar broker-managed funds.

Also, brokers are still paid "trailing commissions": As long as you stay invested, they continue to collect a fee (deducted from your return, of course), whether they get up in the morning or not. Further, we can't help wonder: If brokers have truly gone straight, why are also-ran in-house funds still close to 50% of most brokers' sales?

Complexity

Who needs it? Sales loads needlessly complicate investing. At one time, the decision was simple: You bought a load fund from a salesperson, or you bought a no-load fund on your own.

No-load competition has forced load fund distributors to concoct a bewildering array of front loads, back loads, 12b-1 fees, and share classes—all in the name of flexibility. This "flexibility" has made fund investing much more confusing, and we wouldn't be surprised if many of the no-load deserters have gone over the hill just for simplicity's sake. Who needs to pay extra for complexity, particularly since it does nothing to improve returns? Trying to find your way through the fee maze diverts time and energy from what should be your emphasis: the quality of your investments, asset allocation, and risk.

Lack of Flexibility

The human condition subjects us to all sorts of unanticipated events, some of which require changes and not the least of which involves simply changing your mind!

Morningstar's Publisher, Don Phillips, on Fund Fee Complexity*

"It's sad that so much talent and energy has been applied toward gimmickry designed to fatten management's wallet, rather than toward creating superior returns for investors. That the mutual-fund concept has withstood and even flourished during such tinkering doesn't alter the facts: These tricks undermine the reputation for quality upon which the fund industry is built. As money managers invent new ways to lower the flow of information to investors, while simultaneously raising the costs of their services, they jeopardize their franchise. No one questions the merit of diversification or of professional management, but at some point the value of any service can be outweighed by its cost." (April 3, 1992)

*Morningstar Mutual Funds, Morningstar, Inc., Chicago, Illinois, 800-876-5005.

Often overlooked is how much flexibility you lose by investing in a load fund. If you want to get out of a front-end load fund soon after investing, the decision is difficult because the load takes a chunk out in a short time rather than being amortized over a number of years. An early sale of a back-end load fund is probably more bedeviling because the penalty gets smaller as times goes on. You have to agonize about whether you should postpone redeeming and for how long.

When better alternatives are available, both arrangements are unsatisfactory. Why should you be penalized for changed circumstances or simply changing your mind about your own money?

Conversely, what happens if you're happily invested in a load fund and you get bad news about it? Management companies merge, get taken over, raise fees, and merge other funds into yours or vice versa. Portfolio managers get transferred to other funds, get hired away, quit, retire, start their own funds, and occasionally depart for that big boardroom in the sky.

Where does that leave obedient shareholders who find themselves owning something quite different from what they bought?

In many cases, you're in the soup. You pay a penalty if you change your mind, but it doesn't work the other way around. Fund managers can change—or change their minds—but there is one iron-clad rule on Wall Street: No refunds!

How Much Does a Good Feeling Cost?

Even though it may "feel" better to buy a load fund, there is almost nothing to recommend it. The best approach to fund investing is one that offers:

* Lowest costs that carry the highest probability of superior returns

* Unbiased advice, if any
* Unrestricted selection
* Simplicity rather than complexity
* Maximum flexibility

The only "extra" you get with sales load funds is advice. However, much of it is suspect, biased, or just plain bad, which is worse than no advice at all. Load funds fail to measure up to any of the other criteria, but no-load funds fill the bill quite nicely.

Having heard the cases against individual stocks and against load funds, you would think that managed no-load funds would be the answer for the individual investor. So it would seem. However, they are not for a couple of very good reasons.

Rear-View Mirror Investing

The hardest thing in life is which bridge to cross and which to burn.

David Russell

"Past performance is not a guarantee of future results." This is probably the most often repeated sentence in all mutual fund literature—and the most widely ignored. Investors and professional advisors select funds more for past performance—investing by what they see in the rear-view mirror—than for all other reasons combined. Any skepticism you have about the dominance of past performance as the primary selection criterion can be cured by glancing at mutual fund literature or advertising.

Unfortunately, numerous studies have shown that basing fund selection on past performance doesn't work. We identified the top ten performing funds of all stock funds, regardless of category, for the ten-year period ending December 31, 1985, as listed in the 1986 edition of

Wiesenberger Investment Companies Services (now called CDA/Wiesenberger*):

1. Fidelity Magellan Fund
2. 20th Century Growth
3. Lindner Fund
4. Quasar Associates
5. Evergreen
6. 20th Century Select Investors
7. American Capital Pace
8. Sequoia Fund
9. Pennsylvania Mutual
10. Mutual Shares

It is interesting to see how the top ten performed the following decade:

Total Annual Return—January 1, 1986 to December 31, 1995	
1. Fidelity Magellan Fund	17.42%
2. Quasar Associates	15.82
3. Sequoia Fund	15.45
4. Mutual Shares	14.99
S & P 500 Index	**14.88**
Vanguard Index 500	**14.58**
5. 20th Century Growth	14.23
Average Return	**13.66**
6. Lindner Fund	12.30
7. Evergreen	11.84
8. 20th Century Select Investors	11.77
9. American Capital Pace	11.52
10. Pennsylvania Mutual	11.28

Four out of ten beat the S&P 500 and the Vanguard Index 500 Fund, but the average return of the ten trailed

*Copyright © 1996 CDA/Wiesenberger.

those bogeys. Only one of the previous decade's top three stayed a winner. Had you been lucky enough to own the four ten-year winners, you would have beaten the index fund by only 0.91% annually, compared to the four worst which lagged by 2.98%. The reward was less than one-third the amount of the risk.

A much broader study was reported in *Bogle on Mutual Funds*. John Bogle identified the top 20 equity funds (excluding concentrated specialty and international funds) in each year during the 1982 through 1992 period, along with their results for the following one-year and ten-year periods.

One-year results: "Funds in the top 20 ... on average, ranked 284 out of 681 funds in the subsequent year. While better than mere chance—which would suggest an average rank of 341—it can be described as regressing to the mean."

Ten-year results: "The average rank of the top 20 funds in the first decade fell to 142 of 309 funds in the second. While that is slightly higher rank than the median rank of 155 that was achieved at random, the difference is certainly statistical noise."

His conclusion: "... investing in the winners of the past, solely in terms of highest relative return ... does not appear to increase your chances of selecting the winners of the future."

The unpredictability of future returns is not limited to mutual funds. As far back as 1968, a study of institutional portfolio returns by Michael Jensen in the *Journal of Finance* found that returns were random regardless of previous track record. *Investment Advisor* (September 1994) reported on a study of 144 institutional equity portfolios over rolling ten-year periods between January 1, 1975 and December 31, 1989, and another study updated the results to 1994. Both studies showed that, "... once again, [results] appear to be entirely random."

Investors who have failed to pick winning funds using past results should not be embarrassed. They are in very good company. In our opinion, *Forbes* has consistently provided the best mutual fund coverage by any magazine. Each year they pick an Honor Roll that excludes sector funds. Their eminently logical selection criteria are:

* Evaluation of past returns in both up and down markets for at least ten years
* Funds still open to new investors
* Continuity of management for at least five years

We can't come up with more logical selection criteria. Nevertheless, the results have been uniformly discouraging to fund pickers. A study of Honor Roll funds' returns done by an investment consulting company of rolling five-year periods (1980–1984 and 1986–1990) revealed that in aggregate, they outperformed the S&P 500 Index only once in seven years. Even more disheartening was the fact that in none of the studied periods did they beat both the S&P and the average equity fund.

One-year results provided little encouragement: Honor Roll funds lagged both the S&P and the average equity fund seven out of eleven times. Overall, both the S&P and the average stock fund beat the average Honor Roll fund for both one- and five-year periods.

John Bogle's book examined the returns of Honor Roll Funds from 1974 to 1992. His findings are shown in Exhibit 2-2.

Wall Street's version of the Oscar is a five-star rating by *Morningstar,* the most widely quoted mutual fund tracking and advisory service. *Morningstar*'s risk/reward rating system includes historical measurements and performance time weightings for three-, five-, and ten-year periods. A 1994 Lipper Analytical Services study showed that, in each of the prior four years, equity funds that had been award-

Exhibit 2-2. Honor Roll funds compared to average equity funds and the total market.

	Average Annual Return	Cumulative Return	Final Value of Initial $10,000 Investment
Honor Roll funds	+11.2%	+650	$75,000
Average equity fund	+12.5	+843	94,000
Total stock market*	+13.1	+936	103,000

*Wilshire 5000 Index (adjusted for 0.20% annual expenses)

ed *Morningstar*'s five-star rating underperformed their respective asset class average return over the ensuing 12 months.

Despite overwhelming evidence and actual experience showing that it doesn't work, rear-view mirror fund selection is still the most common practice. The final outcome is predictable: random results. Putting the past behind you is often a good idea. It's a *great* idea in picking mutual funds, because there's no future in it.

Why Mutual Funds Run Out of Gas

Most of the time I don't have much fun. The rest of the time I don't have any fun at all.

Woody Allen

The widely accepted notion that this or that portfolio manager is the prime mover of a successful fund is not supported by the evidence. Why, then, do some funds hit it big, some miss altogether, and others just sputter out after a run of success? When an above-average mutual fund runs out of gas, it doesn't come to a dead stop. It simply drops back into the pack with all the average and below-average performers. There's not a lot of reason for fanfare.

When a fund is outperforming most of its competitors, however, it isn't a secret for very long. The financial press makes sure everybody knows about it, and, in case not everybody is listening, the fund cranks up its advertising. If it's a load fund, brokers and distributors are on the horn to their customers because it is so much easier to sell a hot fund than a cold one. If the stock and bond market is doing well, large amounts of money flows in; if the market is doing very well, titanic amounts pour in.

Thus money chases, rather than anticipates, exceptional performance.

Being in the Right Place at the Right Time

This is the result of thinking in a linear fashion. We think that whatever has been happening is most likely to continue, and the longer something continues, the more confident we become. For example, after decades of rising prices, anyone expressing reservations about lofty California real estate prices in the late 1980s was a candidate for ostracism. Anyone trying to sell their homes at the inflated prices of the late eighties in the midnineties would be similarly isolated.

Markets do not accommodate linear thinkers by going in a straight line forever; they move cyclically—up and down. Cycles sabotage the plans of linear-thinking investors who typically invest in hot funds late in the game, just as they are about to turn tepid or even cold.

What linear thinkers don't realize about mutual funds is that most above-average funds usually happen to be at the right place at the right time. When whatever they have been doing cycles into popularity, above-average returns materialize because they have been managed in a certain style or concentrated in a certain sector all along.

Managing with an investment *style* refers to the basic methodology or rationale of the fund manager. It is what makes a fund "tick." The two broadest style categories are growth and value.

* *Growth style* investing means that the portfolio manager favors stocks of companies that he or she believes will grow faster than the economy. Growth investors are hoping that there won't be disruptive changes and that their companies will continue to grow rapidly, which will in turn provide above-average returns.

* *Value style* fund managers typically invest in depressed and unpopular stocks. They can be "big uglies"—large lumbering companies with undervalued assets—or small companies ignored by most institutional investors. Value investors are betting on change, that their obscure companies will eventually be discovered by institutions or that their big companies will be restructured, managed better, or acquired by another company.

While value and growth investors take different paths, both are trying to get to the same place: above-average returns.

In addition to investment style, many managers concentrate in certain industries or *sectors*. To use the jargon, they "overweight" sectors such as technology, energy, or health care, believing that they will do better than others.

Most academic studies have shown that investing in funds whose style or sector concentration is out-of-fashion is more profitable than those that are in vogue. But the financial press and brokers concentrate on what is in fashion because their audience is most interested in what's happening today, not yesterday or even tomorrow.

Most funds run out of gas because their style or sector concentration cycles from popularity back to unpopularity.

Where the Deals Are

It is not unusual for a large fund family to funnel "hot deals" into one or two of their smaller funds to boost returns, which in turn attracts more investors. If you have wondered where the hot deals that you couldn't get from your broker go, this is the place. If the IPO market cools or management diverts hot deals to other funds, the turbocharged performance ceases.

Performance can also suffer if the fund's assets increase to a size at which hot deals can't have much impact. The boost from hot deals makes management seem better than it is, and the apparent performance is almost never sustainable for long periods.

The Problems With Success

Fund performance can stall for reasons that have nothing to do with portfolio management, but rather with structural problems of the fund management business. One of the most bedeviling problems is size. When an above-average fund gets a huge influx of cash, the portfolio manager suddenly has more money than compelling ideas, particularly if the fund's performance has been built with small-cap stocks.

With money cascading in, the fund has to make larger and larger trades that impact prices when it buys and sells. It can prevent them from buying some stocks altogether. As SoGen International Fund's legendary manager Jean-Marie Eveillard admitted, "When we were at $200 million to $300 million, we could accumulate $500,000 of a small stock over time. Now at $1.8 billion, we wouldn't even bother. If the stock doubles or goes to zero it won't be noticed...."

Seldom do managers of swollen funds acknowledge a conflict of interest. The huge influx of money means a pay raise of historic proportions. Some small-cap managers claim they can handle the problem by including more stocks in their portfolio. But this rings hollow; the manager who is wildly enthusiastic about 40 stocks is unlikely to be equally enthusiastic about 40 more. Some funds, recognizing the size problem, have closed to new investors.

Still Paying the Fiddler, Even After He's Gone Home

Most funds that have closed to new investors because of size considerations have discontinued charging 12b-1 fees, which are deducted from shareholder returns to pay for "distribution and marketing costs." Since there is no marketing or distribution, dropping the fees is only logical. However, we discovered a fund that had closed with well over $1 billion in assets that still extracts 0.25% annually. While that might not sound like much, it amounts to over $3.5 million a year assessed against shareholders—payment for services *not* rendered. Lesson: Shareholders beware.

Size creates another problem. If an exceptional fund manager brings in more staff and hands over part of the management responsibilities, the odds are slim that new recruits are similarly gifted. A bigger staff can also reveal that the brilliant portfolio manager may not be an equally talented people manager. As in any business, trying to manage hypergrowth is distracting and time-consuming, and deteriorating fund performance often results.

While the iron's hot, the temptation to launch new funds to capitalize on success is almost overwhelming. It is hard to resist bringing in "just" another $1 billion because this would bring in another $7 to $10 million in annual management fees. This, of course, creates even more management responsibilities.

Success causes another problem: Exceptional managers are hot commodities in the fund management industry. They can be hired away or start new firms—one of the reasons management turnover runs around 10% a year.

Chasing hot funds is exciting in the short term, but over the long run, it is usually self-defeating. It carries a hazard: Bear markets are cruel to just-before-the-top investors. Even worse, if you pay sales loads to switch funds, each time there is less left over to invest. Results are likely to be dreadful.

> *Even God cannot change the past.*
>
> Agathon
>
> Is it true, as you might suspect, when a "hot" manager exits, performance suffers? A study by CDA/Wiesenberger* concluded that it does. Their ten-year study showed, "that a change in management does more than just negate the significance of a track record; it reverses it. Strong-performing growth funds whose manager left were far more likely to wind up with below-average performance in the period that followed than were strong performers whose managers stayed."
>
> *Copyright © 1996 CDA/Wiesenberger.

Above-average funds are usually their own undoing because remarkable performance forces many undesirable changes, many beyond the control of the portfolio manager. These changes are unlikely to turn above-average performance into even more above-average. More likely, returns will regress to the mean or below it. The fund just runs out of gas.

The Dark Side of the Moon: Mutual Fund Masochism

> *Statistics are like a bikini. What they reveal is suggestive, but what they conceal is vital.*
>
> Aaron Lowenstein

Ironically, even when funds are at the top, shareholders might not be prospering as much as you would think. A sea of statistics tells us precisely how well most mutual funds have behaved, but how about the investors in those funds? How have they shared in the bounty?

Unfortunately, other than a small number of studies that didn't get much press and that aren't easy to get hold of, almost no information is available on how well the average fund investor has been doing. The few studies that have been done show that investors' bad behavior has caused mediocre results at best and, for most, dreadful returns. Investors can't blame brokers or funds; much of the damage is self-inflicted. The few studies available indicate that the average investor checks into funds after they soar and checks out after they bomb.

One of the earlier alerts was a *Forbes* article in February 1988. It showed the difference between time-weighted (fund) returns and dollar-weighted (average investor) returns of the two hottest funds at the time, Fidelity Magellan and 20th Century Select:

	Annual Return December 31, 1977 to December 31, 1987	
	Time-Weighted	*Dollar-Weighted*
Fidelity Magellan	31.0%	13.4%
20th Century Select	24.3	11.5

Forbes commented:

Magellan's dollar-weighted performance over the decade was an astonishingly low number.... Who's to blame? Not [portfolio manager Peter] Lynch.... The fault is the investing public's, with its typically ill-timed rush into the market after the party was mostly over.

The most inclusive study of fund investors' returns we found was one done by DALBAR, Inc., of Boston. Their ongoing study covered the period January 1984 through December 31, 1995. Their findings reported that average investor returns were as follows:

Market Segment	10-Year Returns (%)
1. S&P 500	460.45
2. U.S. Treasury bonds (long-term)	366.39
3. Corporate bonds (long-term)	345.26
4. Small-cap stocks	258.30
5. Intermediate bonds (Treasury)	227.11
6. Sales force bond funds	161.87
7. Direct market bond funds	130.98
8. Sales force equity funds	114.08
9. U.S. Treasury bills	103.17
10. Direct market equity funds	97.92
11. Sales force money funds	75.71
12. Direct market money funds	73.24

Source: * DALBAR, Inc.

DALBAR's Major Findings

* Investment return is far more dependent on investor behavior than on fund performance. Investor return for the 12-year period ranged from 98 to 114%, compared to 460% for the S&P. The difference is attributable to poor market timing and the fact that money does not remain invested for the entire period.

* Sales force–advised investors outperform direct market investors by over 16% in equity and 30% in fixed-income funds. The advantage is directly traceable to longer retention periods and reduced reaction to changes in market conditions.

* Trading in mutual funds reduces investment returns. The "buy and hold" strategy outperforms the average investor by more than three to one after 12 years.

* More investors are making the wrong choice about the method of investing in mutual funds. The market share of assets in direct market funds has increased in segments where direct market investors perform worst, and has declined where market investors perform best.

* Recent investor behavior shows a trend toward more stable markets. Investors' behavior has been to buy when markets rise and sell when there is a decline.
* This pattern has diminished since 1990 and is replaced by less volatile behavior.

DALBAR's final finding is that fewer investors are trying to out-time the market. While this last finding provides a sliver of hope, a discouraging aspect of the study is how "backward" investors' actual experience was: Due to poor timing, higher-returning stock funds returned less than lower-returning bond funds. Even more disheartening was the finding that average fund investors didn't do much better than they would have in T-bills or money market funds: Average returns were less than one-third of the market indexes.

We hasten to point out that broker-sold (sales force) funds did slightly better than no-loads (direct market) funds due to the higher retention rates of sales force fund advisors, as stated in the study. The question is whether investors felt handcuffed by sales loads, or their brokers influenced them to do the right thing.

Don't make the most common mistake—trying to time the market—which has resulted in such uniformly poor results, as shown by these studies. The superior results shown by funds compared to the returns of investors in those funds is largely the result of the fact that the funds stay pretty fully invested all the time. That's their job. Individuals, on the other hand, procrastinate, delay, or rationalize, cleverly dart in and out of the market, or just "watch for a while until things are more certain." (Were things ever "certain" at any time during the twentieth century?) Meanwhile, months turn into years and years into decades, and Mother Market rolls on and on, through good times and bad, delivering good and sometimes very good returns to long-term investors.

Sadly, most investors capture only a fraction of the market's returns because of their preoccupation with the short term.

Stock portfolios, load funds, and no-load funds all require the type of active management at which most do-it-yourselfer investors are not good. The reason might be the lack of time, the lack of investment savvy, or just a tendency to overreact to market fluctuations. Whatever the reason, most amateur investors—like most professional investors—find it very difficult to beat the market. What to do? If you can't beat the market, join it. The next chapter explains how to do that with index funds.

3

How and Why Index Funds Work for the Investor

There has been an explosive growth of mutual funds and other financial institutions in recent years. It has resulted in a swarm of portfolio managers, computer nerds, analysts, strategists, traders, economists, and consultants roaming the canyons of Wall Street. There are an estimated ten security analysts for every stock listed on the New York Stock Exchange. There are over 8,000 mutual funds, plus banks, bank trust departments, insurance companies, money management firms, and major pension funds—all competing in the money investing business. Add to that the legions competing for their business at brokerage and consulting firms, and you have a medium-sized army. Each and every one is striving for above-average results. They are an impressive bunch—very bright, intense, well educated, highly motivated, and flanked by eager staffs of diligent assistants. Surrounded by banks of computers and state-of-the-art communications equipment, they can be in touch with each other or any market in nanoseconds.

The activities of hundreds of thousands of people with billions of dollars worth of electronics are still governed by the law of averages. It is extraordinarily difficult for any one of them to get very far ahead of their competitors, and even harder to stay ahead for very long. With the wired, roaring crowd always close at their heels, all these pursuers of the Holy Grail—above-average returns—believe that they will find it.

There must be a simpler way.

Nuts and Bolts: How and Why Index Funds Work

We have had two great experiments in the 20th Century....
One was socialism, the other is active fund management.

Rex Sinquefield

An *index fund* is a portfolio of stocks and bonds that duplicates its target index, such as the S&P 500. While an index is a mathematical calculation, an index fund holds the actual securities in the same proportion as the index. It doesn't take a huge staff of high-priced talent to duplicate the holdings of a widely published index—just a few bright folks at a computer working in well-lit rooms.

Index funds are identical to other open-end funds with one major structural difference: They seek only to match the returns of an index (average results), as opposed to the more traditional approach of trying to beat the index (above-average results). Index funds are therefore said to be *passively managed,* while traditional funds are actively managed.

Index fund portfolio changes are few. If more money comes into the fund, more securities are bought, and if money leaves, securities are sold. If a stock in the index is merged, taken over, liquidated (or implodes), the index publishes the change, and the portfolio is adjusted accordingly.

Without a complete understanding of how indexing works, investors might be concerned that indexing is just more Wall Street gimmickry, like portfolio insurance or the misuse of derivatives (which blew up in investors' faces). Precisely the opposite is true because an index fund is mechanically driven. Almost all the other products sold to investors are subject to human judgment, error, and emotion.

Index funds work *with* the market rather than trying to beat it. The investment game is no different from any other measurable human endeavor. If you add up the individual results of all the competitors and divide that sum by their number, you get their average results. While there are always a few individuals at the edges of the bell curve (way above or way below average), the closer you get to the center, the more participants cluster at the "bulge" with average or nearly average results.

The Toll of the Bell Curve

As has happened in the mutual fund business, the more you increase the number of competitors (which statisticians call "the sample") and the number of people measured, the closer results conform to the normal distribution of return (see Exhibit 3-1). Wall Street pros have a term for this phenomenon: market efficiency. The more efficient the market is, the more most competitors are destined to achieve average or nearly average returns.

This poses two vexing problems for actively managed funds:

* First, although fund investors have been led to expect above-average results, the law of averages mandates that, *before* costs, portfolio returns of most funds are going to be average (index) or nearly average. See Exhibit 3-2.
* Second, *after* costs, final returns are going to be below average because marshaling all those expensive Wall Streeters and electronics doesn't come cheap. See Exhibit 3-3.

(text continues on page 51)

Exhibit 3-1. Normal distribution of returns.

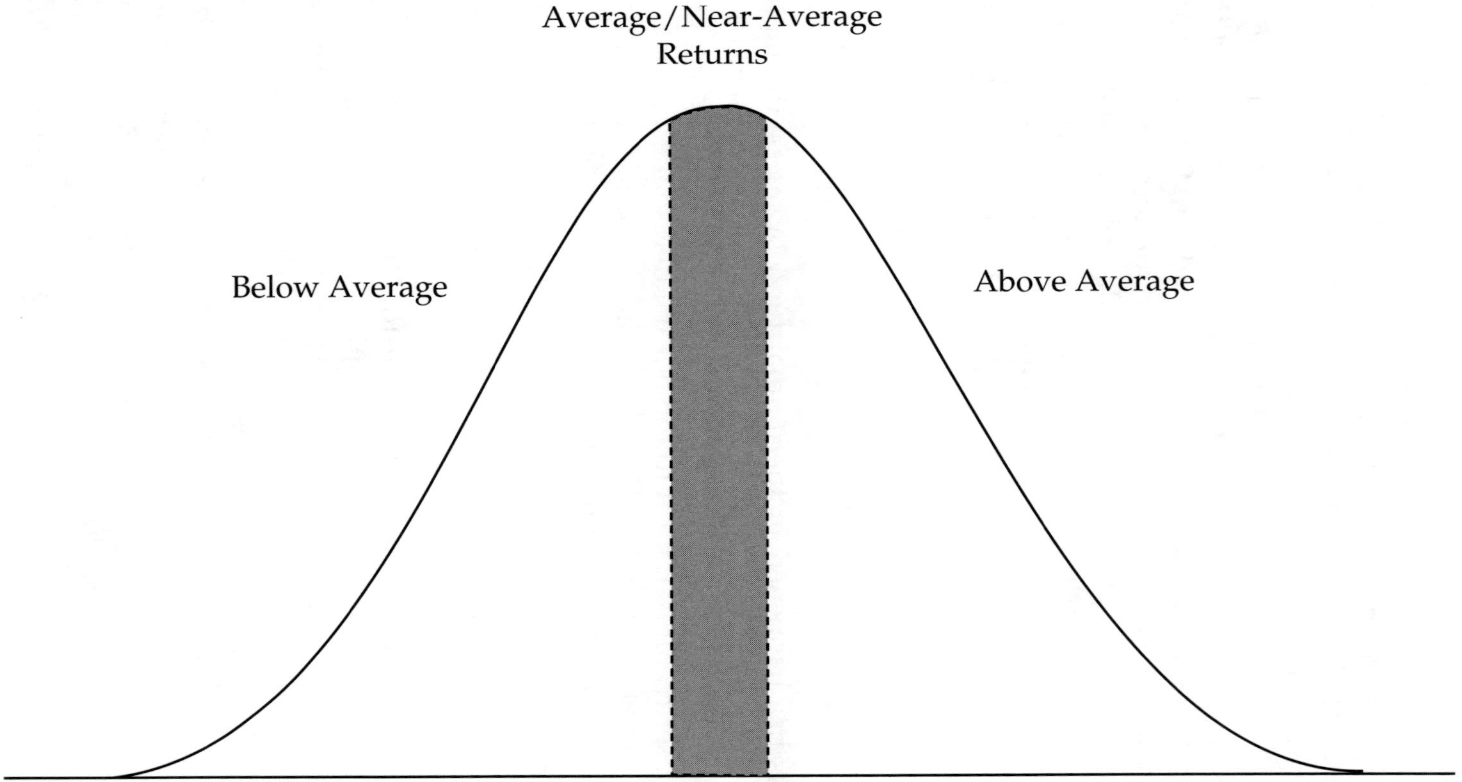

Average/Near-Average
Returns

Above Average

Below Average

Exhibit 3-2. Returns before costs.

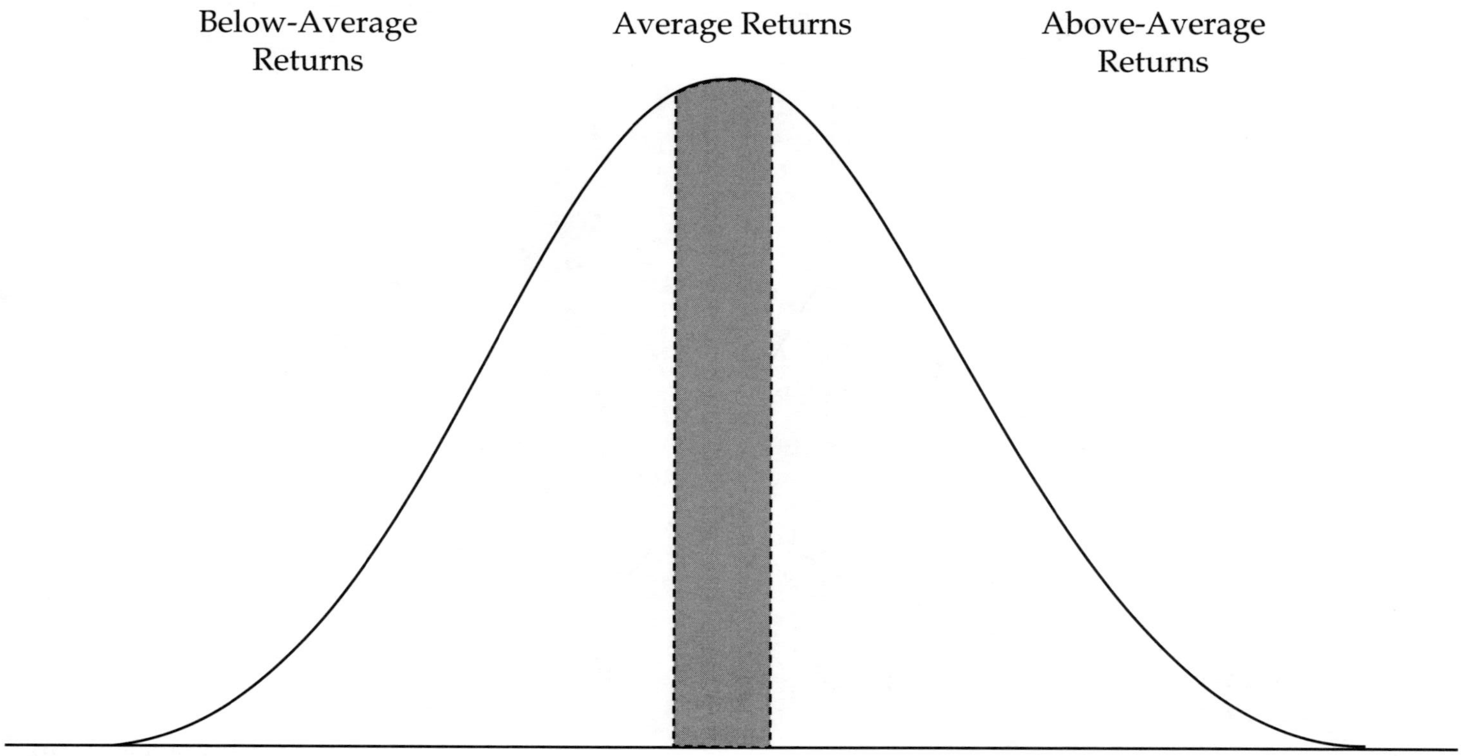

Below-Average
Returns

Average Returns

Above-Average
Returns

Exhibit 3-3. Returns after costs.

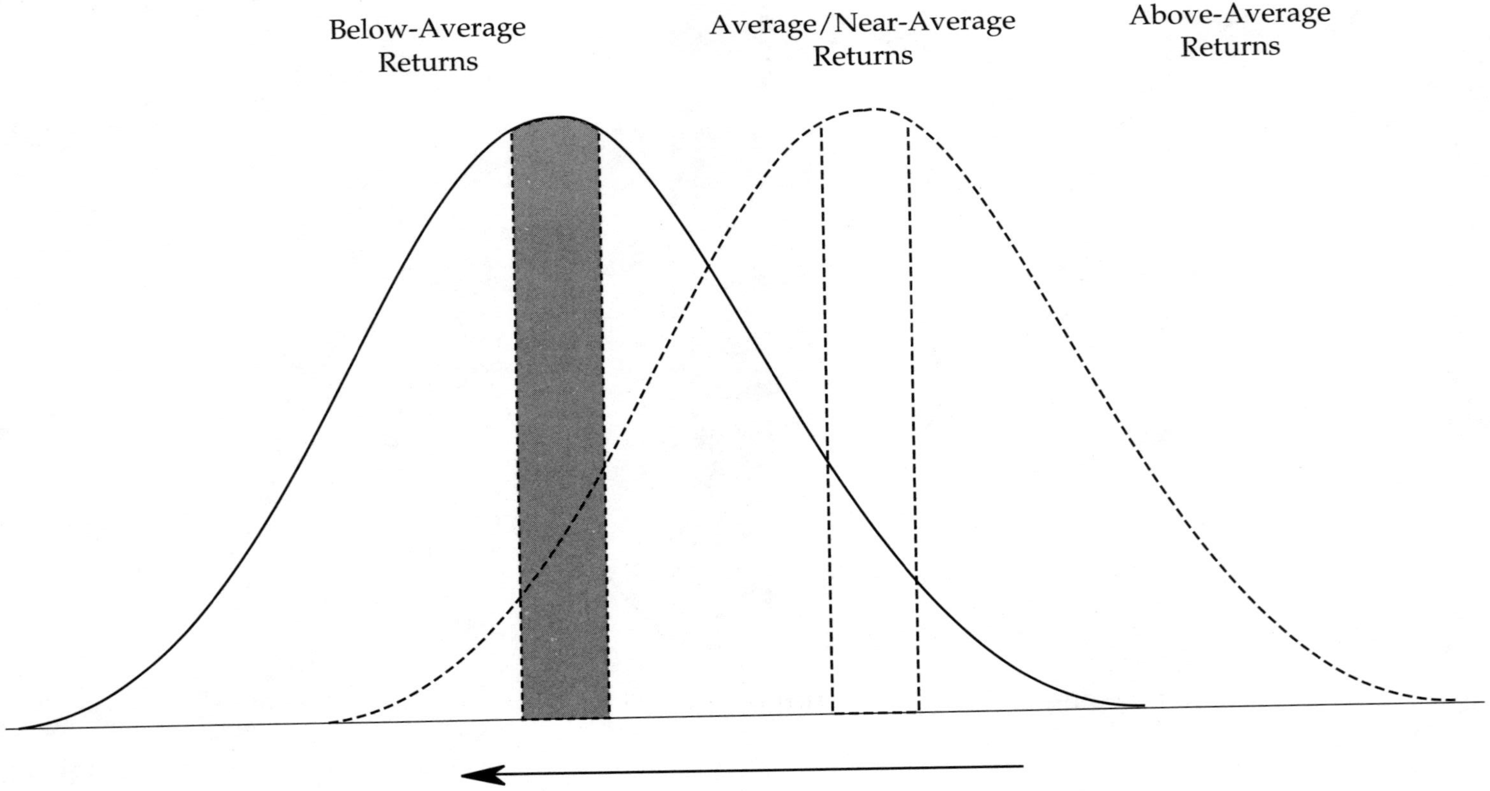

Above-Average
Returns

Average/Near-Average
Returns

Below-Average
Returns

Every January 1, fund shareholders start out the year with only one certainty: They will pay their fund's operating cost and invest only what's left over. How much is left over is determined by the amount they pay in costs. The inevitable results:

* Funds with average or near-average portfolio returns (most funds) produce below-average returns. See Exhibit 3-4.
* Funds with below-average portfolio returns produce shareholder returns that are even farther below average. See Exhibit 3-5.
* Only those funds with portfolio returns high enough to cover costs and also to provide additional return produce above-average returns to shareholders. See Exhibit 3-6.

The net result is that shareholders of most managed funds continue to receive below-average (below-index) returns.

If shareholder returns exceed index returns, active management has indeed provided added value. If returns are average or near average, there is no added value because shareholders have, in effect, paid "something for nothing." If shareholder returns are below average, management is in the uncomfortable position of trying to explain why returns were worse than if there had been no management at all.

Their explanations just don't make sense. As an example, in its annual report for the year ending September 30, 1995, one of the largest fund families explained to shareholders why their growth fund's ten-year return was $39,076 compared to $44,428 for the S&P 500. Identical explanations were provided to their technology ($34,187), utility ($28,290), and income ($29,390) fund investors.

Of course, such unmanaged indices have inherent performance differentials in comparison with any fund.

(text continues on page 55)

Exhibit 3-4. Funds with below-average returns.

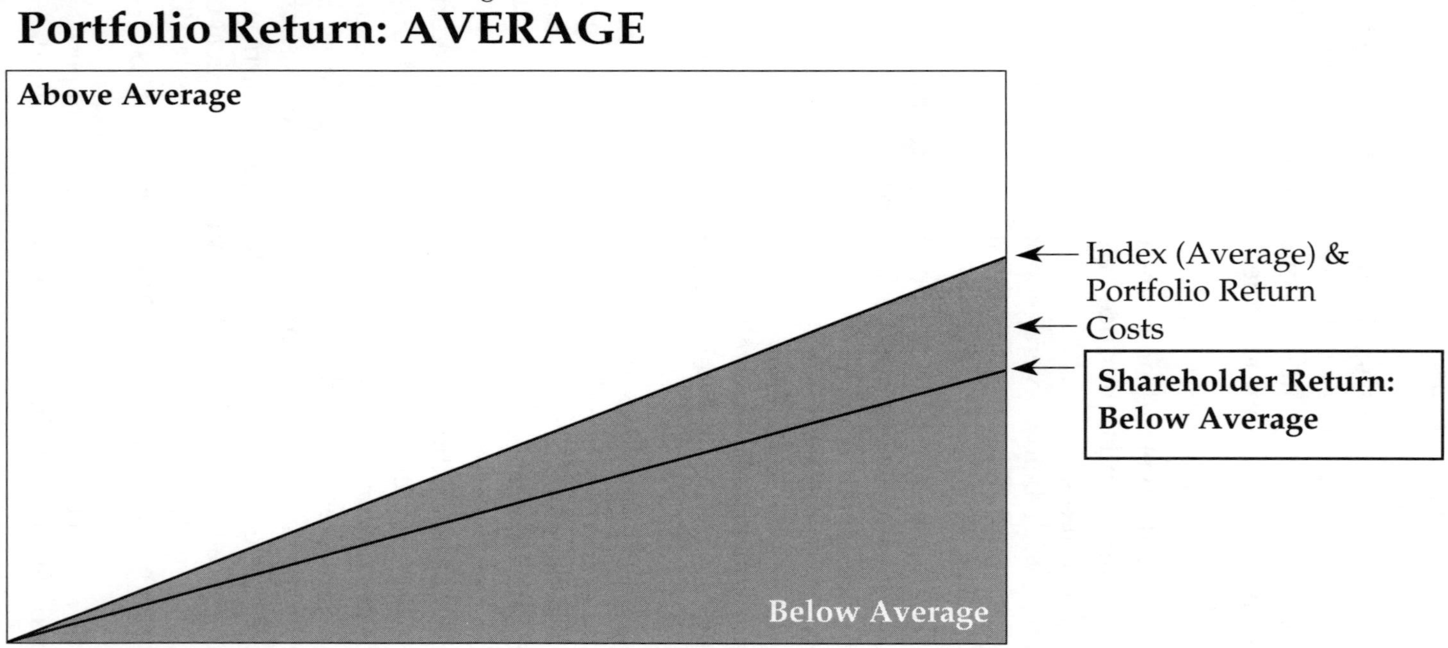

Portfolio Return: AVERAGE

Above Average

Below Average

Index (Average) &
Portfolio Return

Costs

**Shareholder Return:
Below Average**

Exhibit 3-5. Funds with well below-average returns.

Portfolio Return: BELOW AVERAGE

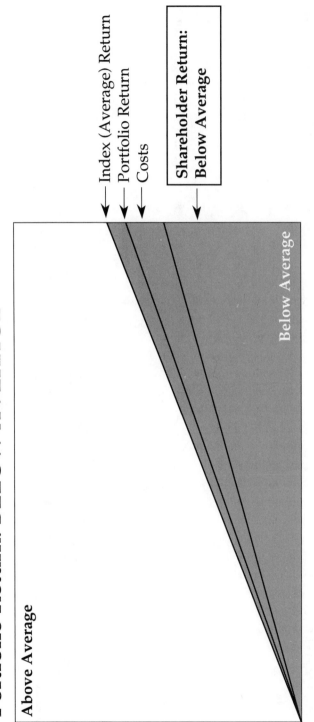

Above Average

Below Average

Index (Average) Return

Portfolio Return

Costs

Shareholder Return:
Below Average

Exhibit 3-6. Funds with above-average returns.

Portfolio Return: BELOW AVERAGE

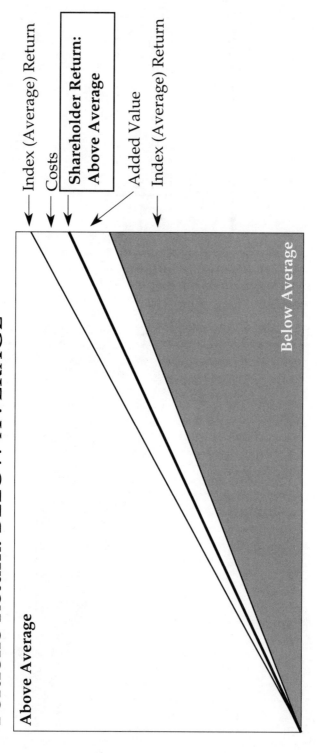

Index (Average) Return

Costs

**Shareholder Return:
Above Average**

Added Value

Index (Average) Return

Above Average

Below Average

They don't pay management fees to cover salaries of security analysts or portfolio managers, or pay commissions or market spreads to buy and sell stocks. And unlike unmanaged indices, mutual funds are never 100% invested because of the need to have cash on hand to redeem shares. In addition, the performance shown for the fund includes the maximum initial sales charge, all fund expenses and account fees. If operating expenses such as [the fund's] had been applied to this index, its performance would have been lower. Please remember that an index is simply a measure of performance, and one cannot invest in an index directly.

While one can't invest in an index directly, it's easy to do the next best thing: buy shares in an index fund. Had one done so (in the Vanguard S&P 500 Fund), ten-year returns would be $42,987, trailing the index by $1,261, but bettering the managed growth fund's results by $3,911—almost 40% of the original investment! Management's explanation is off the mark on another count: They imply that sales charges and operating expenses are inescapable. Of course, they're not; index fund investors avoid them easily.

The Bell Tolls for Active Management

Because shareholders' after-costs returns from most managed funds are below-average, eliminating management must be considered. Replacing a consistently below-average managed fund with an unmanaged index fund is the surest way to improve returns to average or nearly average, resulting in significant increases in returns.

Rex Sinquefield, chairman of Dimensional Fund Advisors, summed up indexing's advantage during a debate at a Charles Schwab Institutional Conference in October 1995. Sinquefield acknowledged the:

allure, the seductive power of active management. After all, it's exciting, fun to dip and dart, pick stocks and time markets; to get paid high fees for this and to do it all with someone else's money.

Passive management on the other hand stands on solid theoretical grounds, has enormous empirical support and works very well for you and your clients.

... Where is the mountain of evidence? The 20th century has produced two grand experiments.... One ... took place on the geopolitical stage and the other in the halls of academia.... So who still believes markets don't work? Apparently it is only the North Koreans, the Cubans, and active managers.

It is clear that the growing body of evidence favoring indexing means that many actively managed funds are living on borrowed time.

The Power of Compounding

Three powerful forces are working for index fund investors and against managed fund investors:

* *Compounding cost savings.* Trying to beat the averages costs the average managed equity fund shareholder around 2% per year. Removing this layer of expense allows the resulting savings to compound. In 15 years, $100,000 compounded at 8% annually increases to $317,722. Add 2% per year and compound at 10%, and it totals $417,772!

* *The law of averages.* Contrary to most Wall Street "discoveries," the more the law of averages is applied, the better it works.

* *The passage of time.* Annual costs savings of "only" 2% may not seem dramatic, but when compounded over time, they mount up to significant sums. The 15-year $100,050 increase shown above, if allowed to compound for just another 5 years, grows to $206,650! Not exactly chump change on a $100,000 investment.

The compelling argument for index funds is that the compounding cost savings, the law of averages, and the passage of time are all working in concert for you year after year. Importantly, they defy human intervention—yours or the professional—and continue to work in your behalf whether you're paying attention or not.

Indexing as All-Weather Investing

There are two times in a man's life when he should not speculate; when he can't afford it, and when he can.

Mark Twain

You want your money to grow and provide income in all kinds of market weather, fair or foul. This can best be accomplished, with the lowest risk, by investing in stocks and bonds of the biggest, strongest, mainstream companies in the United States. If you stray too far afield from quality securities and invest in speculative stocks or stock mutual funds, your portfolio can be very difficult to live with. And you will probably find that you can't live with it during a foul weather period. Investing in mainstream index funds puts you in the best position to weather any storm.

For one thing, when investing in "all-weather" mainstream securities, you're in good company. Institutions (banks, insurance companies, pension funds, and conservative mutual funds) have little choice but to invest in the mainstream. If they get too involved in high-risk investments, they are betraying their legal and moral responsibilities. They face not only damaged reputations, but the loss of clients and even possible legal action.

For the biggest and best companies, the Standard and Poor's 500 Index neatly fills the bill. Started in 1923, it includes a broad spectrum of retailers, high-technology com-

panies, heavy industry, banks, utilities, and service companies, representing approximately 70% of the market value
of all U.S. stocks.

The oldest and best-known index funds are those that
track the returns of the S&P 500. Vanguard Index Trust 500
Portfolio has successfully provided the returns of the S&P
to within one-third of a percentage point for over 20 years.
Because interest in S&P 500 companies by institutions is so
intense, the market is very efficient, and, as just explained,
indexing works best in efficient markets.

By investing in the biggest and strongest companies,
where the largest and most powerful institutions invest
most of their money, you capture most of the profits of that
important segment of the stock market. You also reduce
risks, variables, and worries along the way.

One big reason why index funds work so well despite
market ups and downs is that they take human reactive-
ness out of the decision making. Although it might be hard
to imagine (because of booming stock and bond markets of
the 1980s and 1990s), Wall is not a one-way street. The investing public is more likely to venture out of the mainstream into speculative stocks, and the public can be very
fickle. In bull markets, speculation is exciting and profitable. But when the party is over, profits vaporize as speculative stocks plummet, and the public disappears like a
wisp of smoke from last night's campfire. In falling markets, speculative stocks fall faster and further, and, when
the drop is over, they take longer to recover.

Institutions, however, are perpetual investors. They
don't enjoy bear markets any more than retail investors,
but, like it or not, they are in the game to stay, and the higher-quality stocks they invest in don't suffer as much as
speculative stocks. When the market begins to recover, institutional quality stocks are usually the first to rally.

After a bear market, the public swears off stocks for
long periods and speculative stocks can languish in the
dark cellars of obscurity for years. Risky stocks plummet
far more than high-quality issues, and investors realize

they haven't been investing, but speculating. By then, of course, it's too late to get religion. Many simply sell out and swear off the stock market forever.

In 1974, at the worst, when the market indexes were down 48%, some of the most aggressive small-cap funds were down a numbing 60 to 70%! No matter how philosophical or long-term our horizon, precious few of us are prepared for losses of that magnitude. The greatest risk to speculative fund investing is that the investor gives up and sells out after a big drop. History shows that, with notable exceptions, most speculative mutual funds eventually recover, but what good is that for shareholders who abandon ship at the bottom? The double whammy of locking in losses is that investors forgo any chance of recovering their original investment—and also give up any future profits.

The big lesson is clear: *When the bear ruins the picnic, you are much more likely to stick with your long-term plan if you have invested in a portfolio of mainstream companies.*

Compare the following top-ten holdings of an aggressive small-cap fund (as reported recently) with those of Vanguard's Index 500 fund. As of mid-1995, the small-cap fund was up over 40%, while the index fund was up "only" half that amount.

Small-Cap Fund

Indexx Laboratories	Atria Software
Alternative Resources	Dollar Tree Stores
Macromedia	Global Direct Mail
Gulf South Medical Supply	CRA Managed Care
Storemedia	Adflex Solutions

Vanguard Index 500

General Electric	Philip Morris
Exxon	Merck
AT&T	IBM
Coca-Cola	Procter & Gamble
Wal-Mart Stores	Microsoft

Based on the authors' combined period of more than 50 years in the investment business, during a falling and scary market, we can guarantee that you are much more likely to "hang in there" with Coca-Cola, AT&T, and Exxon than you are with Atria Software and Indexx Laboratories. They may be exciting up-and-comers, but you don't want to be up to your collarbone in unseasoned stocks during a severe bear market.

Even though the average post–World War II bear market has lasted only about 18 months, when you're caught in one, it seems interminable. The six o'clock news reports yet another down day in the market, and the bad economic news piles on week after week like the defensive unit of the Dallas Cowboys. The experts are of little help. Those who were formerly telling you how good things were are now telling you that they are bad.

New experts (those that supposedly forecast the down market) appear, regurgitating their dire forecasts, warming to the subject, and adding even more ominous ones.

And, without exception, just when everything seems hopeless (you've just received your most recent brokerage or mutual fund statement), another genius, whom nobody's ever heard of, publishes an immediate best-seller documenting the hopelessness of it all, explaining why *this time* the investment game is over for good.

We're not recommending how to invest all your money, just most of it. We are not advocating a stuffed-shirt investment plan just to be respectable. We are suggesting an "all-weather" plan that greatly increases the chances of surviving the inevitable downturns in the market. Investing alongside institutions in the strongest companies, in the most cost-effective way, provides most of the returns you expect during good times and enables you to hang in there when times are bad. The beauty of index funds is that they are the most effective in efficient markets where quality stocks and bonds trade. Those are the very sectors in which you should have most of your money invested, even if there were no such thing as index funds.

Proof Positive

You can observe a lot just by watching.

Yogi Berra

Until now, we have not proven the case for indexing. It is time to provide statistics and studies so that there is little doubt left that indexing is the best strategy for mainstream (all-weather) investing.

Hundreds of articles, studies, and comments on indexing have concluded—some without enthusiasm—that index funds beat managed funds most of the time.

> Time to face the cold, hard facts, mutual fund fans: Over the past 10 years, most people would have been better off trading in their actively managed fund for one that tracks the Standard & Poor's 500. Use a long time horizon or a short one—it doesn't much matter. The results are the same. The indexers cleaned up.
>
> —*Barron's* (January 8, 1996)

Detractors (almost always investment professionals) point out that index funds don't always beat managed funds—and highlight instances when they have trailed them. Pointing out exceptions is hardly persuasive. As long as there are only a few, they do nothing to diminish the importance of the rule.

After years of "best" mutual fund cover stories, *Money's* (August 1995) cover story bannered "Why Funds Don't Do Better." The article told readers:

> Small investors turn to mutual fund managers in hopes of superior gains in today's financial markets. Too bad the vast majority of funds aren't able to beat the market averages. A majority of diversified stock funds have been able to outgain the S&P in only 8 out of 20 years from 1975 through 1994 and in just three of the dozen years starting with 1983.

What to do? *Money* recommended that readers invest 45 to 70% of their money in index funds.

Just Compare Indexes to the Best of Managed Funds

Since indexing debuted in the 1970s, there have been many studies of comparative returns that are useful, particularly since all the studies have a "survivorship bias" in favor of managed funds. When a lousy fund is put out of its misery, it is usually merged into another fund, and its poor record magically disappears from the managed fund record books. One study concluded that survivorship bias adds 0.40% to the average annual results of surviving funds.

John Bogle, in *Bogle on Mutual Funds,* cites studies of returns of two of the largest actively managed equity investing groups: mutual funds and pension funds for the 1970 through 1992 period compared to the Wilshire 5000, an index that includes the S&P 500 and virtually the rest of the U.S. stock market.

Equity mutual fund annual returns	+10.8%
Pension fund annual returns	+10.8%
Wilshire 5000	+12.0%

Although there was no Wilshire 5000 index fund in 1970, had there been one charging the typical 0.20% annual expenses, he calculates the return on a $10,000 investment:

Pension & mutual funds	$95,500
Wilshire 5000 Index Fund	$116,300

Bogle also cites a study for a more recent period, covering the results of 205 mainstream mutual funds for the ten years ending December 31, 1992:

Average Annual Returns

Total stock market (Wilshire 5000)	15.4%
Mainstream mutual funds (205)	13.4%

We decided to make comparisons of our own. We selected the returns of Morningstar's Growth and Growth and Income categories because they are mainstream and close-to-mainstream investors. This is not an expedition into the investment wilderness but right into the heartland of mutual funds. Of 1,963 equity funds monitored by Morningstar, 1,367 (70%) fall into these two categories.

Shareholders in the average mainstream fund (the growth and income category) have not been getting returns as high as they would have in a mainstream index fund, as shown in Exhibit 3-7.

The average shareholder has not been receiving index fund returns, and most studies show that their chances of beating index returns are only one in four or one in five. We examined the returns in *Morningstar*'s growth and income category for the ten-year period ending December 31, 1995. Of the 77 managed funds monitored (two additional funds were S&P 500 Index funds), only 16—one in five—actively managed funds beat the Vanguard S&P 500 Index Fund. Note that we compared the S&P with growth and income funds—mainstream funds—not small-cap, aggressive growth, or foreign funds; that would be like comparing apples with oranges (or Buicks). The results are shown in Exhibit 3-8.

We thought it would also be worthwhile to compare Morningstar's growth fund category with the Vanguard Index 500 Fund. While it is a step away from mainstream in-

(text continues on page 66)

Exhibit 3-7. Total returns—Vanguard Index 500 Fund vs. Morningstar Growth and Income Fund average.

	Period Ending December 31, 1995	
Years	Vanguard Index 500 Fund	Morningstar G&I Fund Average
1	37.45%	31.60%
3	15.18	12.97
5	16.41	14.88
10	14.58	12.18

Exhibit 3-8. Morningstar's Growth and Income Fund's 10-year annual total returns.

Rank	Fund	Average Annual Returns
1	Fidelity Growth and Income	19.12%
2	Mutual Beacon	15.64
3	MAS Value	15.47
4	Safeco Equity	15.45
5	Mutual Qualified	15.21
6	Lexington Corp. Leaders	15.13
7	Fundamental Investors	15.12
8	Dodge & Cox Stock	15.03
9	Mutual Shares	14.99
10	IDS Managed Retirement	14.99
	S&P 500 Index	**14.88**
11	Neuberger & Berman	14.86
12	AIM Charter	14.80
13	Massachusetts Invest. A	14.68
14	Washington Mutual	14.63
15	Oppenheimer Total Return	14.61
16	Investment Company of Amer.	14.60
17	**Vanguard Index 500**	**14.58**
18	Putnam Fund for Growth & Inc.	14.57
19	FPA Paramount	14.55
20	Pierpont Equity	14.49
21	Babson Value	14.38
22	Vanguard Windsor	14.37
23	SEI Index 500*	14.33
24	Fidelity	14.10
25	Scudder Growth and Income	13.97
26	IDS Stock A	13.95
27	Merrill Lynch Capital A	13.80
28	Selected American	13.68
29	AARP G&I	13.67
30	Merrill Lynch Basic Value	13.63
31	Affiliated	13.54
32	Dean Witter Dividend Growth	13.48
33	Nationwide	13.41
34	Sentinel Common Stock	13.32
35	IDS Equity Select A	13.22
36	IDS Equity Value	13.19
37	Founders Blue Chip	13.05
38	Alliance Growth and Income	13.04

Rank	Fund	Average Annual Returns
39	American Mutual	13.04
40	Pilgrim Magnacap A	12.88
41	Colonial A	12.78
42	American Leaders	12.73
43	State Street Research Inv.	12.73
44	Salomon Bros Investors	12.65
45	Van Kampen Amer. Cap Comstock	12.65
46	Hancock Sovereign	12.64
47	Van Kampen Amer Cap G&I	12.61
48	Seligman Common Stock	12.53
49	Penn Square Mutual	12.51
50	New England Value	12.33
51	EBI Equity	12.27
52	Vanguard Trustees Equity	12.24
53	Federated Stock	12.23
54	New England Growth & Opport. A	12.23
55	Smith Barney Equity Income A	12.02
56	T. Rowe Price Growth & Inc.	11.88
57	Composite Growth and Income	11.87
58	Pioneer	11.86
59	Hancock Growth and Income	11.85
60	Cardinal	11.84
61	Berger 100	11.83
62	SBSF	11.77
63	IAI Growth and Income	11.61
64	Pioneer II	11.61
65	Burnham A	11.53
66	Winthrop Growth and Income	11.21
67	Strong Total Return	11.19
68	Lutheran Brotherhood	11.17
69	Bartlett Basic Value	11.07
70	Scout Stock	11.06
71	Keystone Growth and Income	11.00
72	FPA Perennial	10.86
73	Dreyfus	10.83
74	Paine Webber Growth and Income	10.52
75	Lexington Growth & Income	10.36
76	Philadelphia	10.19
77	Gateway Index Plus	10.10
78	Analytic Option Equity	9.78
79	Legg Mason Total Return	9.35

vesting, it isn't a huge one. We're comparing not apples and oranges, but more like oranges to tangerines. The comparison should show improvement in the returns from managed growth funds because they take more risk than growth and income funds. They therefore should have provided better results from the strong bull market of recent years.

See Exhibit 3-9. Managed fund returns showed only a slight improvement, particularly in view of the fact that growth funds took more risk than growth and income funds. Even so, in all periods, index funds came out winners. Investors in managed growth funds had somewhat better odds of being in a fund that beat the index fund. Of 121 growth funds, 32 beat the Vanguard Index 500 Fund, two tied, and 87 lagged. So the odds improved slightly from one in five to one in four.

Let's convert the percentages (which may seem remote and possibly academic) to dollars, and compare the returns received by the average growth and income fund shareholder with the Vanguard Index 500 shareholder:

$10,000 Investment
Average Fund: January 1, 1986 to December 31, 1995

Vanguard Index 500	$40,035
Average G&I	$31,561
Index Fund Advantage	$8,474

Exhibit 3-9. Total returns—Vanguard Index 500 Fund vs. Morningstar Growth Fund average.

Period Ending December 31, 1995		
Years	*Vanguard Index 500 Fund*	*Morningstar Growth Fund Average*
1	37.45%	30.83%
3	15.18	12.73
5	16.41	16.20
10	14.58	13.06

As you can see, the index fund provided substantially more return, but that was a comparison against the average growth and income fund.

As we know, there are only three possible investment outcomes: above-average, average (index), and below-average returns. Although it is very unlikely, what would have been the payoff if you had been lucky enough to be in the top five funds (average annual return 16.18%)?

$10,000 Investment
Five Best Funds: January 1, 1986 to December 31, 1995

Vanguard Index 500	$40,035
Five best funds average return	$44,803
Five best funds increased return	$4,768

While it is just as unlikely that you would have been unlucky enough to own the five worst funds (average annual return 9.96%), fairness dictates that we tell the other side of the story:

$10,000 Investment
Five Worst Funds: January 1, 1986 to December 31, 1995

Vanguard Index 500	$40,035
Five worst funds average return	$25,843
Five worst funds decreased return	$14,192
Average best funds payoff	**$4,768**
Average worst funds penalty	**$14,192**

So even when you win the mutual fund derby, the winnings aren't big enough to compensate for the risk that you might suffer the larger loser's penalty, particularly since your chances of ending up a "loser" is four or five times greater, as demonstrated by Exhibit 3-10 from the *Vanguard Index Annual Report 1995.*

Exhibit 3-10. Growth and value funds vs. Index Trust 500 (10 years ended December 31, 1995).

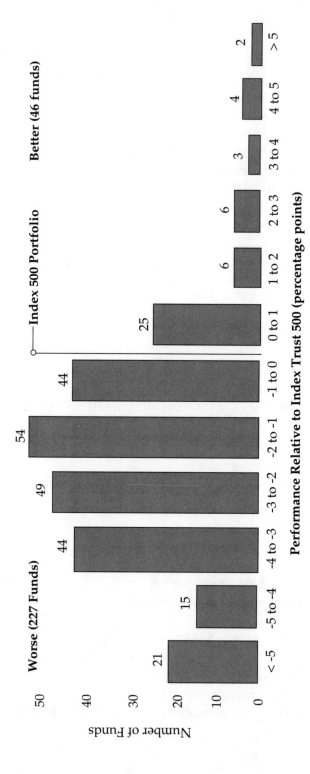

* On average, compared to index fund returns, professional management reduces returns more often than it increases returns.
* On average, compared to index returns, when professional management increases returns, the reward is small compared to the larger penalty when it reduces returns.

The Lessons Learned

What about the future? These figures are historical, and, as we are reminded, "past results are no guarantee of future performance." However, unless they dramatically cut operating costs (expense ratio plus trading expenses), managed mainstream funds' returns are going to trail index fund returns, as they have done historically, by the approximate amount of their costs: 2% annually. Take, as an example, the returns of the Morningstar Growth and Income Fund average, which have trailed the annual return of the S&P 500:

Period Ending September 30, 1995
Morningstar, *November 10, 1995*

Last 15 years	2.03%
Last 10 years	2.85
Last 5 years	1.75

Compelling evidence that indexing works as well in practice as in theory is provided by the graph from Vanguard Index 500 Trust's 1995 Annual Report (Exhibit 3-10). After-cost returns of managed funds form the classic bell curve, and the greatest number of funds' returns, lag the index near their average operating costs: 2%.

Mainstream managed funds are not likely ever to consistently outperform the S&P 500 for another reason: In large measure, *they are the S&P 500.* At the end of 1995, the average fund in the Morningstar Growth Fund Average was 57% invested in S&P 500 stocks. Morningstar's Growth and Income funds had an average of 75% of their portfolios invested in the same group, with some as high as 85 to 90%. Obviously, the probability that these funds can consistently and significantly beat their own portfolios is slight.

Still another reason for managed funds to trail index funds is that most keep a portion of their portfolio in cash equivalents either to meet shareholder redemptions or to take advantage of what fund management perceives as better investment opportunities. Early in 1996, growth and growth and income funds were 7% invested in cash, while index funds had only 2% or less in cash. Over the long term, since the stock market rises more often than it falls, cash investments reduce overall returns. Additionally, managers tend to get pessimistic and build cash reserves in falling markets, usually after they have fallen. Close to important market bottoms in 1974, 1982, and 1987, average fund cash holdings rose to 10 to 11%, which, of course, hurt performance when the market rebounded. In a year like 1995, when the S&P 500 Index returned 37.5%, even average cash positions reduced a managed fund's shareholder returns by over 2%.

The great bull market of the 1980s and 1990s has been so generous that even shareholders in mediocre funds have received bountiful returns. The returns have masked the fact that most of the money investors spend on professional advice and management is wasted and is in fact counterproductive.

Managed fund shareholders are in an ongoing battle with unfavorable odds, and there is nothing on the horizon suggesting that this is going to improve. In fact, if the odds change, they are likely to get worse because the proliferation of new funds leads to even greater market efficiency—in more markets.

The Psychology of Index Funds

Convictions are prisons.

Friedrich Nietzsche

Initially, the premise that indexing improves your mutual fund returns is difficult to accept. To become a convert, you have to change your perception and undergo what has become trendy to call a *paradigm shift*. We don't usually give much conscious thought to our basic assumptions: those we view the world with and how we filter and interpret information—it's "just the way things are."

A paradigm shift is more than simply changing your mind. It means changing your beliefs about the way things are—basic assumptions that you haven't thought about. You are probably unaware that you have most of them.

If you found yourself in Australia—and it had somehow escaped you that the seasons are reversed when you cross the Equator—it would be only natural to plant a Spring flower garden in April. Your long-held belief about the best planting time, based upon your experience of living in the Northern Hemisphere, would be wrong. Similarly, ocean navigation had to have been made considerably easier once the univerally held flat-world theory was replaced with the conviction that the world was round; early explorers no longer had to worry about sailing off the edges of the earth.

Real breakthroughs are not often the result of evolutionary concepts and beliefs; they are usually revolutionary. They provide new and radically changed perceptions of the way things are, and leave traditional thinking—old paradigms—behind.

Several concepts in this book are mind benders, requiring new assumptions and frames of reference:

* No management is superior to professional management.

* Pros cost more than they deliver in terms of increased returns.
* The less you spend for professionals, the better off you are.
* You can improve your returns spending less time, rather than more, on your investments.
* You are going to beat the investment pros most of the time, even though they know a thousand times more about the subject than you'll ever know.

All these notions require a break with traditional thinking.

You Really Won't Sail off the Edge of the World

If indexing is such a "good deal," why have so few investors switched to it? There remain hurdles to large-scale conversion to indexing:

* *Knowledge.* Most investors do not understand indexing. Already largely investment illiterate, only a small minority of investors take time out to do the homework.

* *Psychological appeal.* Initially, indexing appears to be giving up and taking a well-worn path to guaranteed mediocrity. If you can achieve the market-beating returns seemingly so doable with experts' help, why would you settle for "only" average?

* *Indifference.* A *Money* poll (August 1995) of mutual fund investors "showed a remarkable degree of happiness with fund performance: 78% of shareholders were satisfied with their funds' returns of the past year and 82% were happy with their three-year showing." *Money* commented: "it appears that many investors simply aren't paying attention ... this lack of diligence in effect licenses underperformance ... funds don't do better because investors don't demand better."

❊ *Wishful thinking.* Still other factors are investors' (or their advisors') inability to admit mistakes and their tendency to think they are getting higher returns than they are actually receiving. Psychologists call it "cognitive dissonance."

However, reality begs for discovery, and in the shifting paradigm context it is inevitable that investors will realize "the way things are" are in sharp contrast with "the way things ought to be." Then the conversion to indexing will accelerate. As we know, the quest for above-average results by managed funds is counterproductive because managed funds cost more than they deliver. *The seeming paradox is that the simplest, surest, and lowest-cost way is also the way things are.* Fund investors who have felt that they have been on the Wall Street treadmill, and that the treadmill has been winning, can finally get off.

Death and Taxes: Death Preferred

If I could drop dead right now, I'd be the happiest man alive.

Samuel Goldwyn

Since index funds' returns have only started to capture investors' attention, maybe the tax advantages of these investments would raise more interest. If you are investing in a qualified plan that defers your taxes, you don't have to be concerned with current tax liability. However, if you are investing taxable dollars, indexing turns a good story into a great epic.

Like managed fund shareholders, index fund investors are liable for taxes on interest and dividends, whether received or reinvested. But unlike managed fund investors, index fund investors pay less capital gains taxes on their fund returns. Index funds' buy-and-hold strategy means very low portfolio turnover compared to managed funds, who buy and sell stocks more often, subjecting shareholders to annual capital gains taxes. Unless forced to, index funds don't engage in selling, which, in the parlance of the dreary profession, is a "taxable event."

When index fund shareholders die, their heirs get an "income-tax-free step-up" in the "cost basis"—that is, there is no income tax on the difference between the original cost and the value on the date of death. On that day, the heirs' cost basis "steps-up" to the then-current value.

The stepped-up cost basis is no different whether you own index funds or managed funds, but, during their lifetime, index fund shareholders are spared most of the annual capital gains tax that gouges managed fund investors. As a result, indexers have a larger stake to pass on to their heirs.

"It ain't how much you make, it's how much you keep." This old saying is useful in comparing returns from managed funds (how much you make) with index fund returns (how much you make and keep). The tax consideration is particularly important. Even though we hear so much about the impact of pension funds and 401(k) plans on mutual funds, most stock funds are owned by individuals outside of qualified plans, which means that they have to pay federal and state taxes every April.

If you are fortunate (or disciplined) enough to accumulate a significant taxable fund portfolio and are trying to benefit from compounding, naturally you will be reinvesting income and capital gains. The problem is that, while reinvesting compounds your gains, your portfolio doesn't generate any cash to pay taxes on them; you have to subsidize your investment program from your earnings—if you can afford to do so. If not, you are forced to liquidate some of your portfolio to pay taxes. But if you can escape a large portion of the tax liability without giving up returns, as you can with index funds, you are obviously better off.

Lightening the tax load makes a big difference: John Bogle, Vanguard Funds' Chairman, says that for the ten-year period ending in 1994, after-tax returns of Vanguard's Index 500 Fund beat 9 out of 10 of all actively managed U.S. funds.

Tax-Managed Index Funds

So far, only Vanguard offers the recently developed "tax-managed index funds." These funds use various strategies to avoid capital gains distributions, taking the index fund tax advantage one step further. The track record is too short to determine whether the trade-off between tax avoidance and returns is beneficial. Vanguard has a long history of introducing innovative investor-friendly funds, and, if tax-managed funds don't provide positive results, they are likely to do as they have in the past: Fold up a leaky tent and take shareholders elsewhere.

On the other hand, if it does work, as usual, a host of competitors will follow.

If you invest pretax dollars, betting on managed funds against four-to-one or five-to-one odds is dubious at best. When the odds are a dismal nine-to-one (if the ten years ending in 1994 is indicative of future returns), the bet against indexing becomes almost ludicrous.

What Could Go Wrong With Index Funds?

He jests at scars that never felt a wound.

William Shakespeare

Almost all securities suffer during falling markets. Twenty years from now, will we look back to see index funds among the many abandoned hulks rusting in the financial graveyard? Are unseen flaws slowly and insidiously weakening them while they appear to be doing so well? When they hit the next patch of really rough weather, will the wings come off? Will indexes go the way of the billions of dollars worth of limited partnerships of the 1980s? (These disintegrated and led to permanent damage: No amount of patience or steely resolve helped investors.)

Forecasting is a risky business, but we are convinced that, when the going gets rough, index funds will hang tough. Unknowable hazards may be lurking, defying our experience and imagination. Short of that, we are confident index funds are structurally sound and likely to hold up better under stress than many other alternatives and *much* better than some.

The main reason for our confidence has a lot to do with what they are—and probably more to do with what they are not. Fatally flawed Wall Street innovations that ended up in the investment junk yard usually shared common traits, none of which are characteristic of index funds:

* *The heavy use of leverage.* Most of the investment trusts that imploded in the 1929 crash were borrowed up to their eyebrows, as were the failed limited energy and real estate partnerships of the 1980s. More recently, Orange County—California's bankruptcy—and the drubbing of some of the turbocharged U.S. government bond funds in 1994 were the result of investment professionals bulking up with massive debt and then making huge (and wrong-way) bets. Without the megadebt, they would have had a bumpy landing, but they would have flown again instead of being scattered all over the runway.

* *High promotional costs.* Promoters of real estate and energy limited partnerships—now selling at 10 to 25 cents on the dollar—commonly took 20% off the top before their limited partners invested dime one. Exacerbating the problem were hefty annual fees that the promoters paid themselves once the deals were "up and running" (downhill, mostly).

* *Complicated strategies that only the pros understood (or thought they did).* Before the 1987 stock market dive, Wall Street was abuzz with talk about "portfolio insurance" (computer-nerd strategies that protected institutional portfolios from large losses). After the crash, nobody talked about it because in one week it went extinct.

Index funds are free from these afflictions. The plain-vanilla index funds (not "enhanced index funds or wannabes) are unleveraged and uncomplicated. Promotional fees are razor slim. However, as in all areas of human endeavor, index funds are not perfect. There are risks, real and imagined.

Real Risks

Market Risk

Some experts predict that a big percentage of the new mutual fund investors are likely to panic during the next sharp market drop. They envision a downward cycle: novice investors redeeming fund shares in record numbers, forcing funds to sell more and more stocks, causing prices to drop still further, which in turn panics more investors who redeem more shares, and so on. Their scenario has the snowball accelerating down the hill, getting bigger, going faster, and finally ending with a resounding crash. Whether the next market decline is a "crash" or only a mild downturn, if your index fund owns "the market," you will suffer accordingly. Although there are many compelling reasons to index, additional "safety" is not one of them. Compared to other mainstream open-end funds, there is nothing inherently "safer" about index funds.

Index Fund Liquidity

If a steep stock market decline causes many investors to redeem at the same time, index funds don't have much immediate cash to redeem their shares. Compared to managed funds—with cash typically running 5 to 10% of assets, index funds must remain fully invested to match the performance of the index they track.

For investors, there are two major concerns.

First, can the fund reduce its exposure to the market to meet redemptions? As investors redeem shares, an index fund must sell a like amount of securities from its portfolio so that it remains only 100% invested. If the fund's selling lags the pace of redemptions, it will become leveraged, which causes it to experience large price changes than the index it tracks. This is undesirable because the fund's main purpose is to track, as closely as possible, the returns of its target index.

Crystalballing It

It will be no surprise that we'll pass on the idea of joining the tens of thousands of stock market forecasters. However, at this writing, the stock market has had one of the biggest gains, and by some measures, the biggest uninterrupted rise in history. We are probably closer to the end of this cycle than the beginning. Our recommendation: In your planning, if you are going to err, do it on the side of caution.

The second question—one that is probably of immediate concern to you—is whether your check might be delayed if the fund cannot sell fast enough to meet redemptions. Although there are no guarantees, two buffers decrease the chances of delayed payment.

1. The settlement period (the period between when a stock is sold and when the proceeds are received) has recently been shortened to three business days. So stock sales should be able to cover withdrawal checks, which typically take a week or more to clear.

2. Most mutual funds have credit lines available to fund short-term borrowing needs if their cash reserves are depleted. If shareholders bolted from all funds en masse, the huge amount of resulting stock sales would increase transactions costs for all funds. Index funds, however, do not appear to be any more vulnerable than managed funds to this possibility.

The likelihood of an index fund "redemption crisis" is unknowable, as is whether index fund investors might have cooler heads than managed fund investors. There is no history to go on because no publicly held index funds were around during the brutal 1974 market decline, and very few during the 1987 minicrash. The only certainty is that index funds have less of a cash cushion than managed funds.

A possible "redemption crisis" should not be a serious concern of yours because investors invariably panic after the fact (they want out after the big drop). Most importantly, if such a crisis did occur, the problem would be temporary, not chronic or terminal. Once the panic subsides, so do redemptions.

Is Anyone "in Charge?"

This is another go-wrong possibility. The feeling that "nobody's in charge" during stormy weather could unnerve owners of an index fund. An index fund is essentially on autopilot, which is fine in fair weather. When the storm clouds gather, however, the reaction could be like the one in the old Bob Newhart routine when the announcement comes on the airplane PA system: "This is your captain speaking ... captain speaking ... captain speaking ... captain speaking ..." Not very reassuring.

During bear markets, some brokers are able to provide a very valuable hand-holding service to their customers. Others, however, only make their clients feel worse. Think about it: In addition to watching their own investments plunge, brokers are besieged with calls from unhappy customers. The worst part is that they may very well be watching the end of their career; truly bad markets decimate the stockbroker population. Calls to brokers whose lives are passing before their eyes are hardly reassuring.

Even though you don't know when it will happen, or how bad it will be, you have to include the next bear market in your game plan. And for the lack of a starting date, assume that a bear market is coming next week. If you plan for a bear market only after it's all around you, most of the damage is probably already done. Therefore, you have to structure your index fund portfolio so that you won't need a broker or advisor to nurse you through. And you should do that right now.

Imagined Risks

In addition to real risks, there are imagined ones. Despite the recent proliferation of index funds that slice, dice, chop, and puree just about any market, average, or index imaginable, some still think that index funds are only S&P 500 index funds—period. After the next cycle when the S&P lags other indexes, they will undoubtedly conclude wrongly—and loudly—that index funds have failed to deliver as promised. If so, they will have failed to understand that nothing was promised and that the index fund universe is far bigger than just one planet.

Some have wondered what might happen if everybody gets hip and switches from managed to index funds. Imagine it: dark and silent trading rooms ... empty executive dining rooms ... no work for analysts, economists, strategists, traders, and brokers. If most of the market pros are wearing their wingtips in unemployment lines instead of talking to each other on the phone, might the markets lose their efficiencies, causing indexers to lose the advantage they now enjoy?

It will never happen. What's the problem with index funds? "They're no fun," a mutual fund newsletter publisher told *The Wall Street Journal* (February 3, 1996). For many, like going to Las Vegas in spite of unfavorable odds, investing with the guys on Wall Street is "fun." Compared to other strategies, indexing is dull as a door and will never appeal to fun-seekers. Fortunately, there will always be more than enough fun-seekers to keep the index fund game going indefinitely.

Every indication is that index funds will continue to reliably track their target indexes for many years to come. Like all investments, however, they require some thought and planning. The next chapter shows you how to structure your index fund portfolio to maximize returns and minimize risk.

4

Bonds, Bond Funds, and Bond Index Funds

While stock investors invest in the ownership of publicly traded stock issued by corporations, bond investors invest in their IOUs—their debt. Investors can choose from:

* Bonds issued by corporations (corporate bonds), bonds issued by states, counties, cities, and other municipal agencies (municipal bonds), or bonds issued by countries (government bonds)
* Bond funds
* Bond index funds

This chapter explains the pros and cons of each alternative.

Bonds

Gentlemen prefer bonds.

Andrew Mellon

Since 1925, stocks have provided returns of 10% per year, beating inflation (3% per annum) by seven percentage points. Bonds, returning an average of 5% a year, have beaten inflation by only two percentage points.

Compared with stocks over the long term, bonds have been a leisurely disaster. A most compelling case against bonds was made by *Forbes* columnist David Dreman (*Forbes*, December 6, 1993). He pointed out that an investor who invested $100,000 in long-maturity bonds after World War II would have had only $31,500 left in purchasing power, adjusted for taxes and inflation by 1994. Compared to an investment in the S&P 500 (also adjusted for taxes and inflation), stocks returned in excess of $900,000—nearly 30 times more return.

Bonds haven't provided the after-tax and inflation-beating returns that stocks have, but they can't be all bad. Investors own $9.4 trillion worth—more than the $6.5 trillion invested in stocks. Bond funds total just over $800 billion, compared to stock funds' $1.3 trillion in assets.

Obviously, if investors require more current income than stocks or savings vehicles can provide, they have little choice. For them, bonds are almost a necessity. Others should use bonds to generate income and/or to add a measure of predictability and stability to their portfolios.

Bond Risks

The risks associated with bonds are as follows:

* *Loss of purchasing power.* Even if inflation stays at a relatively benign 2.5% rate, you lose half of your purchasing power in 28 years. If inflation moves up to 4%, the period shortens to only 18 years.

* *Investment risk.* The issuer may fail to pay interest and/or principal on time or not at all: default.

* *Market risk.* This is less understood by novice investors: Even though a bond is guaranteed by the U.S.

Treasury, if it is sold before it matures, it may bring more or less than the purchase price. Because bond prices move inversely to interest rates, and rates have fallen throughout the 1980s into the 1990s, bond prices have risen. The easiest way to visualize the relationship is to think of it as a seesaw. See Exhibit 4-1.

In addition to understanding that bonds and interest rates move in opposite directions, it is important to know how far they can move. Sitting very close to the center of the seesaw is analogous to holding a short-term bond. Even if there are large and sudden interest rate changes, you are not greatly affected. However, if you are way out at the end of the seesaw in long-maturity bonds, interest rate changes can result in very large price swings—both up and down. See Exhibit 4-2. A 1% change in long-term rates results in an approximate 15% price change.

Exhibit 4-1. The interest rate/bond price seesaw.

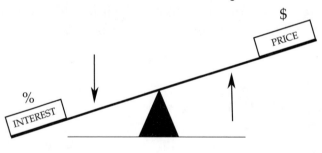

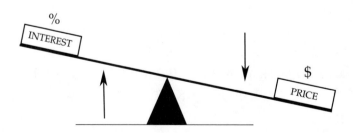

Exhibit 4-2. Price changes resulting from a 1% change in interest rates.

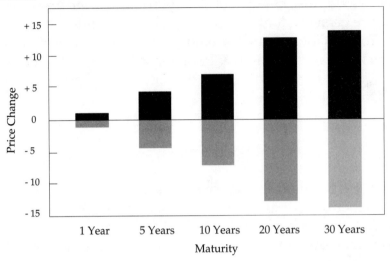

Minimizing Bond Risks

To minimize bond investing risks, invest in high-quality bonds with relatively short maturities. The trade-off, of course, is lower return. But the bond market is *not* the place to look for high, inflation-beating returns; for that purpose, look to the stock market.

Just as most of your equity investments should be high-quality mainstream securities, so should your bond investments. High-quality bonds are desirable because they provide predictability and certainty, and they are the least likely to default. Bond investors who hold until maturity know exactly when they will receive interest (typically every six months) and when they will get their money back (at maturity).

Even with high-quality bonds, shrinking yields over the 1980s and first half of the 1990s have posed a serious problem for income buyers. In the early 1980s, when interest rates were much higher, you could "buy" a $1,000-per-month income stream from U.S. government bonds (yielding 14%) for $86,000. A decade and a half later, with yields having dropped to 6.25%, the same $1,000 would cost you over twice as much—$195,000. As you can see, income buyers have been in a long, losing battle with low interest rates.

You can identify high-quality bond issues by using the ratings services, Standard & Poor's and Moody's. The portfolio quality of a bond fund is disclosed in the prospectus. See Exhibit 4-3.

Bond Funds

In theory, bond investing should be relatively simple: a fixed schedule of payments and a final payback. If you invest in a portfolio of U.S. Treasury bills, notes, or bonds, it is simple. However, if you invest in U.S. government bond funds, it gets more complicated.

Structural Variables

All bond funds share certain structural variables—not all of them good:

* *Possible dilution.* If you invest in a fund in year one, when rates are 8%, and rates fall to 7% in a year or two, new investors' money is invested at the lower rate. The result is that your return drops to less than 8% because you are sharing in the "new" investments at lower rates. You are also sharing—and reducing—your appreciation of the 8% bonds with newer investors. Theoretically, if rates rise, the dilution should work to your advantage because you share in the new money invested at higher rates.

In practice, dilution is more likely to work against you than for you because investors tend to accelerate their investing when prices are rising, and they stop investing when prices are falling. Prior to 1994's sharp bond market drop, investors were piling into bond funds in record numbers. In 1994 and 1995, they went on strike: Net inflows to bond funds were essentially zero.

Exhibit 4-3. Standard & Poor's corporate and municipal rating definitions.

Long-Term Issue Credit Ratings

The issue credit ratings are based, in varying degrees, on the following considerations:

1. Likelihood of payment-capacity and willingness of the obligor to meet its financial commitment on an obligation in accordance with the terms of the obligation;
2. Nature of and provisions of the obligation;
3. Protection afforded by, and relative position of, the obligation in the event of bankruptcy, reorganization, or other arrangement under the laws of bankruptcy and other laws affecting creditor's rights.

AAA	An obligation rated AAA has the highest rating assigned by Standard & Poor's. The obligor's capacity to meet its financial commitment on the obligation is extremely strong.
AA	An obligation rated AA differs from the highest rated obligations only in a small degree. The obligor's capacity to meet its financial commitments on the obligation is very strong.
A	An obligation rated A is somewhat more susceptible to the adverse effects of changes in circumstances and economic conditions than obligations in higher-rated categories. However, the obligor's capacity to meet its financial commitment on the obligation is still strong.
BBB	An obligation rated BBB exhibits adequate protection parameters. However, adverse economic conditions or changing circumstances are more likely to lead to a weakened capacity of the obligor to meets it financial commitment on the obligation.
BB, B, CCC, CC, C	An obligation rated BB, B, CCC, CC, and C is regarded as having significant speculative characteristics. BB indicates the least degree of speculation and C the highest. While such obligations will likely have some quality and protective characteristics, these may be outweighed by large uncertainties or major exposures to adverse conditions.
D	An obligation rated D is in payment default. The D rating category is used when payments on an obligation are not made on the date due even if the applicable grace period has not expired, unless Standard & Poor's believes that such payments will be made during such grace period. The D rating also will be used upon the filing of a bankruptcy petition or the taking of a similar action if payments on an obligation are jeopardized.
Plus (+) or Minus (-):	The ratings from AA to CCC may be modified by the addition of a plus or minus sign to show relative standing within the major rating categories.
r	This symbol is attached to the ratings of instruments with significant noncredit risks. It highlights risks to principal or volatility of expected returns which are not addressed in the credit rating. Examples include: obligations linked or indexed to equities, currencies, commodities; obligations exposed to severe prepayment risk—such as interest-only or principal-only mortgage securities; and obligations with unusual risk interest terms, such as inverse floaters.

Source: Standard & Poor's July 1996 *Ratings Handbook,* by permission.

  * *Shareholder costs.* The efficiency of the bond market means that the correlation between lower costs and higher returns is even stronger for bond funds than for stock funds. Some funds charge as high as 1.5% annually, with typical costs running around 1%. Countless studies have shown that the higher the bond fund expenses, the lower shareholder returns are.

  * *Morningstar* commented on July 7, 1995:

> The first place that Vanguard really made its mark was with high-grade bond funds. By now, most invest-ment-grade managers will privately acknowledge that they can't be expected to keep up with a Vanguard fund.... The investment-grade bond market is too straightforward to analyze and too dominated by ra-tional, informed buyers to overcome Vanguard's head start due to expenses which amount to 75 basis points (0.75%) per year.*

  * *Sales loads.* By now, we hope we are preaching to the choir, but it bears repeating that, just as with stock funds, sales loads reduce the investible amount, thereby reducing net returns.

  * *Unpredictability.* Unlike bond investors who know the timing and amount of their interest and principal pay-ments, bond fund investors can only make educated guess-es as to the amount of interest payments and none about principal. Bond funds have no maturity date. Possible di-lution is a variable, as is the constant change in the portfo-lio. A bond fund with an average portfolio maturity of ten years still has a ten-year maturity eight years after an in-vestor buys it because the manager is continually replen-ishing the portfolio. By contrast, an investor in a ten-year bond knows that, in the eighth year, the principal will be repaid in two years.

*Morningstar Mutual Funds, Morningstar, Inc., Chicago, Illinois, 800-876-5005.

Product Quality Problems

As if the structural variables aren't enough, bond fund investing has been complicated by some fund management companies and broker-distributors. Some of the merchandise has been very good but, unfortunately, it's been mixed in with too many shabby fixed-income products, some bad enough to be included in the nefarious customer-buster category.

Many investors, fearful of stocks, have ventured into investing only as far as bonds, assuming—and encouraged by Wall Street distributors—that they can't go too far wrong because of bonds' relative safety, particularly when managed by investment professionals. It is particularly unfortunate that some of the worst merchandise was sold to the least sophisticated customers: income investors who are typically the most risk-averse. Many bond fund investors fall victim to the same flawed assumptions that undo the average stock fund buyer:

* The pros will outsmart the market and deliver higher returns than investors can get on their own.

* The pros will, by increasing returns, more than make up for their cost.

Sound familiar? The first assumption falls victim to the fact that the bond market is even "smarter" than the stock market. The other fails because on average, just as in stocks, instead of enhancing returns, costly professionals reduce them.

If this weren't enough, to deliver "extra" returns, many bond fund managers have taken far more risk than advertised. Maybe a couple of paragraphs in the fund prospectus say something about increased risks, but who reads the prospectus?

Shabby and Customer-Buster Merchandise

There should be a Hall of Shame for the ill-conceived bond alternatives that ended badly. Among the prominent ones are:

* Construction-lending real estate trusts
* Income oil and gas and real estate limited partnerships
* Option-income funds
* Closed-end bond fund IPOs
* Leveraged closed-end funds
* Enhanced income funds
* Mortgage derivative funds

And so on. Results ranged from mildly disappointing to real customer-busters, some of which resulted in shareholder lawsuits.

In the shabby category are what we call Peter-Paul bond funds. These funds systematically rob Peter's principal to pay Paul's income. Rather than "preservation of capital," as is often promised in the prospectus, slivers of principal are routinely distributed as income. Why? Because many investors want income above all else. As many brokers can attest, "yield sells." Many investors aren't aware that their nest eggs are shrinking each year. Either that or they don't know what to do about it. It doesn't make any difference in qualified plans such as IRAs and 401(k)s, where income is reinvested and not taxed, but for retirees living on distributed income the result is awful. The longer the process goes on, of course, the more inevitable is reduction of income.

Of a number of "sophisticated" techniques for robbing Peter to pay Paul, the most common (which even we understand) is investing in premium (high-coupon) bonds at a premium to face value. This inflates income but dissipates capital, as is shown in Exhibit 4-4. You may not agree that the $3,350 in the example was "lost" since it was inevitable when the investment was made and was partially

Exhibit 4-4. A do-it-yourself Peter-Paul investment.

$10,000 U.S. Treasury 10.25% Due August 2005
Price (February 26, 1996) 133$^{16}\!/_{32}$

Cost	$13,350
Annual income	1,025
Annual cash-on-cash yield ($1,025 divided by $13,350)	7.518%
Yield available on bonds selling at face value	6.100%
"Extra" annual yield	1.418%

The Future
Bond Matures at par (100) August 2005

Amount received	$10,000
Versus cost	13,360
Amount "lost"	(3,350)

---

offset by the higher annual income stream. Agreed: You know it, and we know it, but how many bond fund shareholders know it?

Peter-Paul bond funds are common. *Forbes* (January 1, 1996) listed 14 of the worst, which they called "capital offenders," with assets totaling over $43 billion. During the period October 1986 to September 1994 (a period of rising bond prices), Peter's payout to Paul depleted Peter's nest egg (NAV) by an average 12.4%. NAV erosion ranged from 7 to 23%. By comparison, Vanguard Fixed Income L-T Treasury Fund's NAV *increased* 16%.

All the "big capital eaters" were load funds. This is not surprising since they have less principal to invest and have to do something to boost their income to compete with no-load funds.

Forbes' capital eaters are not no-name funds operating out of Jersey City garages. All but one had "U.S." and/or "government" in the fund name, which would suggest to most simple folks a commitment to preservation of principal. Taxable bond fund investors are among the least sophisticated of all investors, and it is particularly unfortunate that five of the 14 funds don't even include total account value on shareholders' statements. If capital is eroding in a rising market, a falling market is going to cause NAV mudslides.

Going from the shabby to the customer-buster category are funds that take far more risk than advertised. Until the 1994 bond market drubbing, some funds were, in fact, paying "extra income" compared to supposedly similar funds. When the wheels came off, some U.S. government bond funds dropped 20% in a couple of months. Some critics smugly pronounced that naive shareholders, enjoying their free lunch, should have "known better"—that their above-average returns were the result of taking above-average risk. Yet very few shareholders knew that their fund was leveraged and souped-up with inverse floaters, CMOs, mortgage rolls, and the like.

Had they known, why should they have been alarmed? Isn't that the way it is supposed to be? You hire the pros, and they increase your returns. You don't hire a French caterer to open cans of tuna; you can do that on your own. It wasn't the customers who should have known better, but the pros cooking up their exotic derivative concoctions. From now on, extra returns, if any, will probably end up in the lawyers' pockets.

Bond Fund Investing Strategies

As already pointed out, long-term bond fund investing is not a "winning" strategy. Payment of interest and principal are fixed; there are no rising earnings and dividends that ultimately lift prices as they do in the stock market. All but the most horrid stock funds bail investors out eventually. Lousy bond funds just sit there and deliver lousy returns.

Assuming you dodge the booby traps, bond investing can be relatively simple, even though it is not as neat and tidy as it might appear. How much you should allocate to bonds compared to other assets is covered later in the book. Once that is decided, the alternatives for bond investing are fairly clear-cut.

Certainty

If absolute certainty is your highest priority, U.S. Treasuries are the clear choice. There is no danger of your bonds being called (some bond issuers can "call" their bonds prior to maturity and return your money whether you want it or not). Diversification is not necessary because, if Uncle Sam defaults, equal opportunity is sure to prevail for all investors. If you need a monthly income check or if you are willing to sacrifice some yield for convenience, a U.S. government bond fund should be considered. You can buy bonds directly from the U.S. Treasury, thereby avoiding brokerage commissions entirely. See Exhibit 4-2.

Laddering

Since the most volatile price swings take place at the longer maturities as interest rates change, we recommend *laddering* maturities. This is bond-speak for staggering maturities. With staggered maturities, you aren't making a big bet on the direction of interest rates. If you ladder every two to four years, you have some of your bond money coming back to you on a regular schedule. Laddering is not a heroic approach, but the bond market is not a place where legends are made anyway.

Exhibit 4-5. Treasury direct accounts—worth the trouble?

You can buy U. S. Treasury securities directly from the Federal Reserve Bank if you want to escape the small charges (typically $50 to $75) levied by brokers. Once you have established an account, you can buy the following maturities:

* Bills: 3-month, 6-month, 1-year

* Notes: 2-year, 5-year, and 10-year

* Bonds: up to 30-years

The minimum for bills is $10,000. For notes with maturities of less than five years, the minimum is $5,000. For notes with maturities between five and ten years and bonds, the minimum is $1,000. When maturities are met, bids are accepted in multiples of $1,000.

You can:

* Upon maturity, instruct the Federal Reserve Bank to automatically roll over your investment into the next maturity.

* Have interest payments from notes and bonds (after first payment is mailed to you) wired automatically to your checking account.

You cannot:

* Buy, except at scheduled auctions.

* Buy zero-coupon securities.

* Sell through a Federal Reserve Bank. Securities must be transferred to a broker before they can be sold.

To receive the publication describing Treasury Direct Accounts, call the Federal Reserve Bank in your area.

Costly convenience ...

While investors have placed over $100 billion in government bond funds, do they realize how much return they are giving up for the sake of convenience? While annual expenses of around 1.0%-plus (counting funds' trading costs) may not sound like much, it amounts to a very substantial 15% reduction in income: $100,000 invested directly in U.S. government *bonds* will provide $1,000 more annual return than a typical U.S. government *bond fund*. If bond investors light their cigars with five $100 bills every six months, they will end up with about the same net return as bond fund investors.

Other Do's and Don'ts of Bond Fund Investing

* *Don't* pay sales loads—front, back, level, or any other form not yet dreamed up.
* *Don't* invest in bond funds promising "extra returns."
* *Don't* invest in bond funds with long average maturities, unless you have to for cash flow. The bond market has been benign for more than a decade, and a protracted bear market would be very damaging to bond fund investors. Exhibit 4-5 shows just how much. A 1% increase in rates would cause 20-year bonds to fall over 10%.

  For reference, it is useful to compare current rates with those of the early 1980s when long-term rates were 14 to 15%, and money market rates were flirting with 20%. Clearly, most of the current interest rate decline is behind us. We are simply running out of arithmetic. Generally, we would not recommend going beyond ten-year maturities at the very most. The additional return doesn't compensate for the increased market risk.
* *Don't* invest in bond funds with high expense ratios.

* *Don't* put more than 10 to 20% of your total bond allocation into high-yield (junk) bond funds because, in many ways, junk bonds' market risk is comparable to that of stocks.
* *Do* "ladder" your bond fund maturities for the same unheroic reasons recommended for U.S. Treasuries. Even though you won't have money coming due periodically, it dampens the volatility of your bond asset allocation. Laddering also allows you to stretch your longest maturities a bit because your average maturity is somewhere about half the longest maturity.
* *Do* include bond index funds.
* *Do* consider corporate and municipal bond funds to increase returns using the same selection parameters recommended.
* *Do* keep it simple. Bond professionals love to dazzle us with minutia. If an alternative seems too complicated to understand, it's probably too complicated to invest in.

Bond Index Funds

Question:	*What should a man never do in the presence of a woman?*
Answer:	*Yawn.*

Frank Sinatra

Bond index funds came late to the bond fund party. Vanguard launched the first one in 1986. In theory, bond indexing should work even better than stock indexing since the bond market is more efficient than the stock market. In actual practice, indexing does work better.

For the five-year period ending December 31, 1995, the Vanguard Bond Index Total Market Fund had an average annual return of 9.27% versus an average 8.15% for the 220 comparable funds tracked by *Morningstar*. We are using a Vanguard Index fund once again because, having been around the longest, it provides the most information. As you might expect, a good part of this advantage comes from Vanguard's lower operating costs. Their expense ratio is 0.18% versus 0.72% for its peers, and the portfolio turnover ratio (remember that trading costs also reduce returns) averaged 38.4% the last five years, less than one-third of its average competitors' 129.4%.

Vanguard's 1.12% average improvement in returns may not seem like much compared to the average 2% advantage provided by stock indexing until you compare it with the arena in which it operates. The bond market is so efficient that it is very difficult for a bond fund portfolio manager to add value. How many ways can a U.S. Treasury or high-quality corporate bond be analyzed? The biggest variable, therefore, with similar bond funds (comparable quality and average maturity) is cost, and here, of course, indexing shines. We have belabored the importance of cost so much up to now, we will spare you citing additional studies confirming the importance of costs. If you're not with us by now, you never will be.

Although the bond indexing improvement is a smaller increment compared to stock indexing, when compared to return—rather than to the amount invested—indexing's advantage is even higher than for stocks. See Exhibit 4-6.

Exhibit 4-6. Total average return.

	Five Years Ending December 31, 1995			
	Managed Funds	*Index Funds*	*Advantage*	*Advantage as Percentage of Return*
Stocks	14.88%	16.41%	+1.53%	10.28%
Bonds	8.15	9.27	+1.12	13.74

Morningstar Mutual Funds, Morningstar, Inc., Chicago, Illinois, 800-876-5005.

Of course, there are drawbacks. While indexing improves bond fund investing, it still has the inherent disadvantages of bonds in general and the structural difficulties of bond funds.

Even though we are indexing advocates, we should point out that Vanguard's managed bond funds have such low costs that they also should be considered along with index bond funds. For example, while the Vanguard Index Fund Total Bond Market Portfolio expense ratio is 0.18%, the expense ratio of their managed Fixed-Income Long-Term Corporate Bond Fund expense ratio increases to only 0.32%—an increase of only $14 per $10,000 invested. Including Vanguard's managed bond funds increases your selection possibilities.

Bonds are your anchor to windward. You may depend on them for income, but, when considering bond and bond fund alternatives, do as Confucius counseled: "When in doubt, do that which you will least regret."

Until now the focus has been largely on what does not work or on what doesn't work as well as index funds. The next few chapters look at how index funds can be put to work in your portfolio.

5

Asset Allocation

Wall Streeters might not quarrel with being compared to trusty airline pilots who deliver trusting passengers to chosen destinations. A more accurate comparison, however, is to small pilot fish (Naucrautes ductor) that follow sharks and are so named because they only seem to be piloting. The pilot fish owes its existence to shark leftovers, and there's probably no doubt in the shark's mind or the pilot fish's who decides where they are going and when.

Despite decades of promotion suggesting otherwise, markets "run" the professionals; professionals don't run markets. The markets decide where the pros are going, and the pros clearly live off market leftovers. It can be a fatal mistake if you believe otherwise. The pros do fine tuning—some good, some bad—and much reporting and explaining, but if Mother Market heads off in any direction, the best the pros can do is just hang on.

You Bet Your Assets

We have two classes of forecasters: those who don't know—and those who don't know they don't know.

John Kenneth Galbraith

The Most Important Principle in This Book

Asset allocation   the division of assets among stocks, bonds, sub-categories within those markets, and cash—dwarfs all other investment considerations.

If you are invested in rising markets, the chances of your success are very high even if you are invested ineptly. That is, even if you pay too much for investment professionals who underperform the market, the rising market bails you out.

But, if you make a big wrong-way asset class bet, you are in serious trouble because you are continually trying to swim upstream. Even the most savvy professionals have great difficulty making any progress under these conditions. No matter how talented they were, no long-term bond fund managers were able to avoid the systematic ruin exacted by the 30-year bond bear market that ended in the early 1980s. Interest rates on the rise from 3 to 14% drove bond prices down and down again. Just when they seemed as though they had stopped going down, they went down still more. Similarly, stock fund managers during much of the 1970s didn't do so hot either: Stocks went "nowhere" while real estate prices soared and money market yields approached 20%. (The sick joke at the time was that, when interest rates hit 20, they would split 2-for-1.)

The gold market is a fine example of being in the wrong place at the wrong time. Over the last 15 years, while mainstream stocks (the S&P 500) provided an eight-fold return on investment, a $10,000 investment in the average *Morningstar*-tracked gold fund returned a pathetic $10,277! The very best gold fund's (Franklin Gold One) returns were better, returning 5.11% annually, but it still trailed the S&P 500 by the huge margin of 9.29% a year.

However, gold isn't always a bad asset; in the not-too-distant past it soared from $35 to $800 an ounce, and, as recently as 1993, the average gold fund was up 84.9%!

As a result of your own experience, you already "know" the importance of being in the right asset at the right time. There were times to have been in real estate in the 1970s and times to have been out in the 1990s. If you had any kind of half-decent stock or stock fund plan in the last 15 years—even if you entrusted your fate to overpaid, underachieving pros—your returns, though below-average, were probably still pretty good.

Nothing's permanent. The decade of the 1970s was just the opposite; it included the worst stock market break since 1929 in 1973 through 1974. Stock investors suffered while money market "investors" were coining it.

The most often quoted study of the importance of asset class selection was of 91 large pension funds over a ten-year period.* The conclusion: The vast majority (94%) of a portfolio's returns variance is determined by asset class selection, and only a small portion (6%) by market timing and stock selection. This study raises once again the issue of whether most of the money spent on traditional active portfolio management (market timing and security selection) is wasted, since it has such a small effect on returns.

Academic studies confirm our experience *that asset class selection is monumentally more important than any other investment consideration.* Indexing, whose primary function is to replicate various asset classes, is the natural solution to the asset class selection "problem"—as long as it can reliably replicate the desired asset classes. The task of choosing between a relatively few asset classes compared to

*Gary P. Brinson, L. Randolph Hood, and Gilbert Beebower, "Determinants of Portfolio Performance," *Financial Analysts Journal* (July-August 1986), pp. 39–44; and Gary P. Brinson, Brian D. Singer, and Gilbert L. Beebower, "Revisiting Determinants of Portfolio Performance: An Update," 1990, working paper.

thousands of stocks or managed funds is less formidable, but you are still faced with hard choices:

* Which asset classes should you invest in? Which should you avoid?
* Of those selected, how much do you invest in each? Once you are invested, do you make changes?
* If so, when?

Asset allocation and indexing are not sure-fire solutions to all your investment problems. If you load up on index funds in the right asset classes, you'll win big. Unfortunately, predicting asset classes that are destined to soar is no easier than picking tomorrow's hottest stocks.

Even though it still involves hard choices, asset class selection has important advantages:

* *Efficiency.* Time and effort are spent on the most important considerations—those that have the most impact on returns—not wasted on trivial concerns.

* *Perspective.* Asset class investing requires looking at the "big picture" issues of risk and return.

* *Objectivity.* Too often, investors lose objectivity because they "fall in love" with a stock, a company, or a fund manager. Then the market sometimes obliterates the thin line between love and hate, which tends to make things worse. Decision making is made easier because it is hard to love or hate an asset class.

In constructing your fund portfolio, the task is made easier because countless books and magazine articles have recommended "model" portfolios that use the following parameters:

* Years to retirement
* Income needs

* Lump sum or periodic investments
* Risk tolerance
* Future needs

Most of the model portfolios are relatively similar, and although we break little new ground, we will recommend specific portfolio structures. What most seem to lack is that they understate what can go wrong. In our experience, what "goes wrong" most often is the investor, not the plan. The reason is that most investors misunderstand or underestimate the importance of risk.

Pothole Investing

… your ultimate success or failure will depend on your ability to ignore the worries of the world long enough to allow your investments to succeed. It isn't the head, but the stomach that determines the fate of the stockpicker.

Peter Lynch, Beating the Street

You are not a seasoned investor until you've hit a pothole. Once your teeth have been rattled by the likes of the 1973 through 1974 period or the 1987 market drop, you become more preoccupied with risk than before. Fifty years of combined "full service" convinces us that few investors are as prepared for losses as they think. During the next big drop, many of today's brave faces will then look like deer caught in the headlights.

Your challenge is to determine your personal trade-off. How much uncertainty are you willing to endure to increase your returns? While the glass may be half full over the long term, during down markets you may become convinced that it is half empty—or, worse, that you are better off if you just toss the glass.

If you imagine yourself solely invested in stocks during the next "normal" market decline, it will provide some useful reference points. Post–World War II bear markets have fallen an average 30 to 35% and have lasted an average of 18 months. But think not in terms of percentages, but in terms of dollars, because that is what you're concerned with. If your latest statement showed a month-end value of $85,800, down from $132,000, you are likely to be preoccupied with the fact that you have *lost $46,200!* Although your 18-month, 32% loss may be historically "normal," few investors are prepared for this kind of normalcy. *Are you?* Even though everybody "knows" that the market goes in both directions, few prepare for it. Investors who ask why they made $46,200 are rare indeed; those who question why they lost $46,200 are legion.

In a falling market, if the majority of your funds are indexed, there's nobody to blame but Mother Market (and maybe yourself, if you're a bit of a masochist), but she won't be listening. If a drop of over $46,000 causes you to come apart and sell (locking in your losses, like having them bronzed), 100% stock allocation is obviously not for you.

What size loss, then, could you reasonably "live with"? Twenty-five thousand or "only" fifteen thousand? Whatever the amount, convert it to a percentage of your portfolio. If $20,000 is all you can stand, convert it: $20,000 divided by a portfolio of $132,000 is 15%.

We recommend that you construct your own "risk tolerance matrix" (our contribution to Wall Street speak). Factor in your portfolio value and a stock decline that reflects "normal" post–World War II declines of 30 to 35%. This is a crude conversion of art to science, but we are dealing with psychology, emotion, your personal circumstances, and history (which repeats itself but just differently enough each time to keep you guessing).

For all its inexactness, once you have gone through this exercise, you have rough benchmarks to help put things in perspective. You are then in far better shape to weather the next bear market than most other investors. The reason is that most investors seem to have one or both of the following risk management plans, both of which are woefully inadequate to deal with a market that goes up *and* down:

* *Plan 1.* They're going to "watch things [the market and their funds] real close." Many have computerized their investing to watch things even closer. This is a plan to "watch things," not a plan to "do" things.
* *Plan 2.* No plan.

As we saw in the last chapter, when we recommend asset class portfolios, we don't stray far from the stuffed shirt, mainstream stock discipline recommended in Chapter 3. Getting sidetracked into allocating too much to the riskier areas, such as the small-cap stock asset class, is fraught with peril because they can be devastated in bear markets. In the 1969 and 1973 through 1974 drops, the Value Line Index, an index of small-cap stocks, dropped over 50% and 60% respectively. If your planning includes declines averaging "only" 30 to 40%, and your losses exceed your guesstimates by half again as much, your stomach could kick into gear, override your head and cause you to sell near a market bottom.

Suppose that, as in our example, a $30,000 paper loss that brings the value down to $102,000 is about all you can tolerate, and your guesstimate of the magnitude of the next market decline is 35%, a little more than "average." The following matrix shows that you should have no more than 60 to 70% invested in stocks, which we'll round off to 65%.

Portfolio Value: $132,000					
				Stocks Decline	
Percent	*Stocks*	*Bonds/Cash*	*25%*	**35%**	*45%*
100%	$132,000	$0	$99,000	$85,800	$72,600
90	118,000	14,000	12,000	90,420	78,600
80	105,600	26,400	105,600	95,040	84,480
70	92,400	39,600	108,900	**99,660**	90,420
60	79,200	52,000	112,200	**104,280**	96,360
50	68,000	68,000	115,500	108,900	102,300
40	52,800	79,200	118,800	113,520	108,240
30	39,600	92,400	122,100	118,140	114,180
20	26,400	105,600	125,400	122,760	120,120
10	13,200	118,800	128,700	127,380	126,060

This matrix doesn't include fluctuation in the value of your bond allocation. If stocks are dropping, bond prices are probably falling also (because they usually move in tandem). If, however, your bonds or bond funds are high-quality and the maturities are relatively short, their declines will be relatively small compared to the drop in stock prices. Your bond allocation should and will be the least of your concerns.

Unpleasant as this exercise is, as we've mentioned, Wall is not a one-way street. If you aren't prepared for inevitable bear markets, you aren't prepared to invest in stocks. There is no "right" risk tolerance, anymore than there is a "right" shoe size. Only you know what really fits.

6

Picking the Funds

At some point, we stop writing (at another, you stop reading), and we all get on with the business of investing.

The question is how much "investing" do you want to do? Besides risk, income, years to retirement, etc., trade-off considerations belabored elsewhere ad nauseam, another factor is very important and usually ignored: your level of interest. If dealing with investing is akin to doing your taxes, and watching the TV test pattern is preferable to tuning in to "Wall $treet Week," you don't have to be ashamed. Just admit it. You might be characterized as the "indifferent investor," but you are in good company.

Indifferent investors don't necessarily make bad investors; many make the best investors. More fortunes are made by indifferent investors who just "let it be" than by those who feel they always have to "do something"—tinkering with their investments. Constant portfolio meddling—the assumption that you can improve on market returns—is the antithesis of index investing. Indifference is better: While you aren't doing anything, the managements of the companies in your indexed portfolio are. If you "own" the S&P, you have 500 managements, in their own self-interests, striving to increase sales and profits, beat their competition, develop new products and markets, and do all the other things that companies "do." While not all are going to be successful, most increase the value of their companies and their stocks. Book value, earnings, and cash flow are compounding, dividends are increasing, and ultimately all that activity has an impact on stock (and your mutual fund) prices. If your level of interest is higher than indifference, all the better. You get some enjoyment from the process of investing.

If you're absolutely fascinated, be careful. Brokers love to sing the siren song about how they can outsmart Mother Market, and, at the very least, they encourage you to hum along. If you become an active investor ("broker-speak" for stock trader) the odds are very high that the final chorus will be the same old sad song of too few profits after too many transactions.

Bringing It on Home: The Tweddell/Pierce Master Model Portfolio

Money will come if you're doing the right thing.

Michael Philips

Our plan is The Tweddell/Pierce Master Model Portfolio. Despite its title, it is simply a benchmark that serves two purposes:

* It provides a beginning frame of reference—a starting point for you—to plan your own portfolio.
* It provides a continuing frame of reference. As years pass and markets cycle up and down, it enables you to rebalance—to keep you on track with your original plan.

See Exhibits 6-1 and 6-2. Up to age 26, we feel that anyone who is lucky enough to have money to invest at that age should invest entirely in stock funds. The stair-step progression that follows in six-year periods gradually in-

Exhibit 6-1. Benchmark master model portfolio asset allocation.

Age	Percent Stocks	U.S. Large-Cap Stocks	U.S. Small-Cap Stocks	International Stocks	Percent Bonds
20	100%	60%	20%	20%	0%
26	90	54	18	18	10
32	80	48	16	16	20
38	70	42	14	14	30
44	60	36	12	12	40
50	50	30	10	10	50
56	40	24	8	8	60
62	30	18	6	6	70
68	20	12	4	4	80
74	20	12	4	4	80
80	20	12	4	4	80

creases bonds and decreases stocks until age 68, when bonds are 80% and stocks are down to 20% of the portfolio. We can't bring ourselves to invest totally in bonds, and some studies have indicated that a bond/stock ratio of more than 80/20 actually increases risk.

For efficient large-cap stock and bond markets, we strongly advocate index funds because the verdict is in: It is very unlikely that they can be beaten consistently with active management. If you have enough capital and/or want absolute predictability with bonds, substitute a portfolio of U.S. Treasuries for the indexed bond funds. The indexed percentage (shaded in Exhibit 6-2), starting out at 60%, increases gradually as the portfolio evolves to less risk and volatility—and more income.

If you are 38, and a big down day in the stock market has you staring at the ceiling at 3:00 AM, don't just lie there and suffer. Reduce the stock fund allocation from 70% to a level where you can get a good night's sleep. If, on the other hand, you are approaching retirement and have always believed in stocks, you may have no interest in "retiring your money" in bonds; if so, adjust accordingly.

Exhibit 6-2. Benchmark asset allocation model.

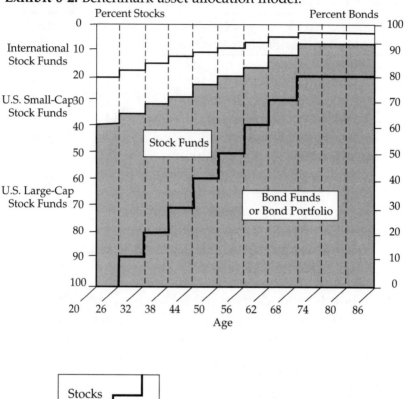

Obviously, adjustments have to be made for the human condition: children's college expenses, obligations to care for an aged parent, inheritance or pension fund distributions, and all the other events that mess up even the niftiest plan.

If you are investing a large lump sum, we recommend that you cost-average in. Invest one-sixth of this amount, consistent with your allocation every six months, so that you are "on track" at the end of three years. If the stock market takes a 30% dive before you're fully invested, don't decide to "watch" or "wait because things are so uncertain." That is the classic time-honored way not to invest. Take advantage of the drop and accelerate your investment schedule.

In Chapter 8, we will recommend specific funds for each allocation. The recommended funds will include index funds for large-cap and bond investment, and both index and managed funds for small-cap and foreign investment.

Putting It All Together

Once you've made the most important decision—asset allocation—you have to select funds for each category. We recommend index funds for two categories: bonds and U.S. large-cap stocks. Remaining are small-cap stocks and international stocks. You have to decide whether to use index funds for those categories or to also include managed funds.

Bonds and U.S. Large-Cap Funds

These are the easiest asset allocations.

Recommended Bonds/Bond Funds

* *U.S. Treasury securities.* Laddered maturities seven- to eight-year maximum maturity

Or a 50/50 split between:

* *Vanguard Short-Term Bond Portfolio*
* *Vanguard Intermediate-Term Bond Portfolio*

U.S. Treasuries are attractive because they are totally predictable as far as payment of interest and principal, and they involve no expenses or costs if purchased directly from a Federal Reserve Bank.

The Vanguard funds—both index funds—are slightly less attractive due to the inherent uncertainties of bond funds (Chapter 4), but they are extremely cost-efficient, particularly for reinvesting income. The short-term fund has an average maturity of 2.4 years and yields 6.39%. The intermediate fund yields 7.09% with an average maturity of 7.5 years.

If your income from these recommended bonds and funds fall short of your needs, you have to make the best of the situation and downgrade bond quality and/or extend average maturities. Our recommendations—again, only if you must—are the following funds:

* *Vanguard Bond Index Total Bond Market Portfolio* seeks to replicate the performance of the Lehman Brothers Aggregate Bond Index: average credit quality AA, average maturity 8.8 years; approximate current yield 6.86%.

* *Vanguard Long-Term Bond Index Portfolio* invests in a portfolio to match the Lehman Brothers Mutual Fund Long Government/Corporate Index: average credit quality AA-1, average maturity 21.3 years; approximate current yield 7.34%.

If it appears that you need tax-free income, consider municipal bonds/bond funds for the bond allocation, but only if your tax advisor concurs. It is remarkable how many people (against the advice of their CPA) are misinvested in municipals because "escaping" taxes has so much emotional appeal. Their after-tax returns are lower than if they owned taxable bonds. Stick with higher-quality, short to intermediate maturities and funds with the lowest expenses. Research the Vanguard and Fidelity Spartan funds, and you shouldn't have to look much further.

The easiest selection is for the U.S. large-cap stock asset allocation:

* *U.S. Large-Cap Stock—Recommended Fund:* Vanguard Index Trust 500 Portfolio

No surprise here with the oldest and biggest S&P 500 index fund's return for the ten years ending December 31, 1995: 14.58% versus 14.88% for the index. Other S&P 500 Index fund candidates are the Fidelity Market Index and T. Rowe Price Equity Index Funds, but expense ratios are higher (0.45%)—than Vanguard's 0.20%, causing returns to lag slightly.

Annual 5-Year Returns
for Period Ending December 31, 1995

Vanguard Index Trust 500 Portfolio	16.41%
Fidelity Market Index	16.23
T. Rowe Price Equity Index	15.99

U.S. Small-Cap Stocks

If you enjoy the investing process at all, this is where you should get your kicks. Most studies have shown that over the very long term, small-cap stocks have delivered higher returns than large-cap stocks. In addition, savvy fund managers have a decent shot at taking advantage of the inefficiencies of the small-cap market. So if you hit a sweet spot, your chances of beating the market improve considerably (with a commensurate increase in risk, of course). Here you can immerse yourself in Wall Street lore: the investment styles, concepts, methodologies, personalities, corporate cultures, and track records of hundreds of funds and the folks who run them.

However, small-cap fund investing is more difficult than it might seem. In a utopian investment world, a well-run managed fund that is a good investment ought to remain so for the foreseeable future. But it isn't so for small-cap funds for the reasons spelled out in Chapter 2: Extraordinary returns breed a whole host of problems that reduce returns.

The problem we face in recommending funds for the small-cap asset allocation is that many we would have recommended previously have already had growing pains or they have closed to new investors. So as not to be burned by a flash in the pan, we set the following criteria. Recommended funds should:

* Have a long-established management company or a portfolio manager with an identifiable track record.
* Have small and manageable total assets.
* Earn returns close to or exceeding its target index and similar funds.
* Experience no excessive portfolio turnover.
* Charge reasonable costs and expenses.
* Not have strayed far from its stated objective/ category.
* Not appear to be overly dependent on IPOs.

Initially, we found one that fit the bill, T. Rowe Price Small-Cap Value, and plugged it in our small-cap slot. Less than a week later, the fund closed to new investors. A return to the drawing boards produced another fund about which we were only slightly less enthusiastic: T. Rowe Price New Horizons (asset size was somewhat of a problem). Apparently we weren't the only ones concerned about asset size because shortly after its selection, it too closed.

Until the stock market cools off, fund closings will continue to plague anyone who has to wait six months to see their recommendation in print. Rather than recommending still another fund that is probably just as vulnerable to closing, we are recommending a number of funds under the generic label of "managed small-cap fund," which you can choose from. They are listed at the end of this section, with comments on why we feel they are attractive (we are retaining T. Rowe Price New Horizons because it has a history of closing and reopening). Not all recommendations are perfect small-cap fits—one of the main reasons we didn't recommend them in the first place. Some own international stocks, and some have "asset drift" into mid-cap and large-cap stocks. And, of course, some may close before this book appears in print.

If you are not inclined to picking a managed fund, simply invest the whole allocation in the Vanguard Index Small-Cap Fund. You could do a lot worse. Vanguard Index Small-Cap Fund has a 1% transaction fee upon purchase. This does not bother us because the fee covers transaction costs, and benefits fellow shareholders rather than being siphoned off by management. In addition, the extremely low expense ratio (0.25%) more than makes up for the 1% transaction fee, compared to the 1.58% average expense ratio of the 366 small-cap funds tracked by Morningstar. It is more than made up for in the first 90 days after investment.

Recommended U.S. Small-Cap Stock Funds

* Managed small-cap fund—50%
* Vanguard Index Small-Cap Fund—50%

International Stock Funds

Our recommendation is a managed fund: T. Rowe Price International Stock Fund.

T. Rowe Price management has a long history of successful international investing. The portfolio manager has been at the helm for over 15 years and the fund is well diversified worldwide with a 16% stake in emerging markets. Annual returns were 14.9% for the ten-year period ending December 31, 1995.

Using our recommended funds and the Benchmark Asset Allocation Model, a 38-year-old investor's $50,000 portfolio would be invested as follows:

30% Bonds	$15,000	U.S. Treasuries
42% U.S. large-cap stocks	21,000	Vanguard Index 500 Fund
14% U.S. small-cap stocks	3,500	Vanguard Index Small-Cap Fund
	3,500	Managed Small-Cap Fund
14% International stocks	7,000	T. Rowe Price International Fund
100%	$50,000	

Since the purpose of using managed funds is to outperform the market, the Benchmark Asset Allocation Model portfolio requires that you monitor your managed funds periodically to make sure that they are outperforming the target indexes or at least equaling them. If you won't be disposed to watching managed funds, the last section of this chapter, "Autopilot Investing," presents a completely indexed portfolio.

Recommended Managed Small-Cap Funds

Since professional management is the primary reason for investing in managed funds, the four funds that follow all share management experience and continuity. In addition, the recent performance of these funds has not been bolstered by oversized technology stakes or by the overheated IPO market, which can make distinguishing between talented and just-lucky managers almost impossible.

Here are four recommendations:

1. *Tweedy, Browne American Value Fund.* Founded in 1920, Tweedy, Browne is widely respected within the financial community as a strict value manager with a bias toward small-cap stocks. Tweedy, Browne first offered American Value along with its sister fund, Global Value, in 1993. Portfolio management is by the four partners, three of whom have been with the firm for more than 20 years. Their long-term record running private accounts has shown results exceeding S&P 500 returns. Indications are strong that Tweedy, Browne is unlikely to bring out a host of new funds. Fund assets are very manageable at less than $200 million. Tweedy, Browne has indicated that, if asset growth begins to hamper returns, they might "consider" closing, but gives no assurance that they will do so. This is not strictly a small-cap fund; large-cap exposure is approximately 40%, and international stocks make up 16% of the portfolio. The expense ratio is above average but should decline as assets grow. Telephone: 1-800-432-4789.

2. *T. Rowe Price New Horizons Fund* (now closed). One of the oldest of small-cap funds. Portfolio manager John Laporte has been managing the fund since 1987 and has managed to beat most of his competitors most years. Laporte displays less fervor and more perspective about small-cap investing than many of his peers. In naming him their 1995 Domestic Stock Manager of the Year, Morningstar commented, "Quietly, he has transformed New Horizons from an inside joke to one of the most attractive, consistent small-company funds around." Small-cap exposure is 60% and midcap is 29%. The New Horizons trade-off: Assets are approaching $3 billion, which makes Laporte's job a bit more difficult. Telephone: 1-800-638-5660.

3. *Baron Asset Fund.* Managed by Ron Baron since 1987, the fund has never wavered from its small-cap growth mission. Recently, small caps were almost 70% of the portfolio,

with midcap taking up another 20%. Asset size, although it almost quadrupled in 1995, is still a very manageable $350 million. Baron Asset is no closet index fund. It is not as diversified as most small-cap funds and, since its founding, has beaten the small-cap Russell 2000 index in seven of nine years. If you like to read about your money, Baron provides shareholders with very informative quarterly reports about the fund's major holdings. If you would like to meet your money, he invites managements of some of his fund's companies to make presentations at the fund's annual meeting and encourages shareholders to attend and ask questions. Telephone: 1-800-992-2766.

4. *Royce Premier Fund and Royce Micro-Cap Fund.* Managed by long-time small-cap manager Charles Royce, both funds are about as small-cap as they get. Premier invests at least 65% of its assets in companies with less than $1 billion in stock market capitalization, and Micro-Cap invests in companies with less than $300 million. Since Royce never waivers from his small-cap value discipline, he has to be in two right places at the right time: both small-cap and value. Unfortunately, since launching these two funds in 1991, the market has not gotten in synch with both his preoccupations simultaneously. If it cycles into Royce's microasset niches simultaneously, there could be fireworks. Meanwhile, the fund has been delivering respectable but unexciting returns. Telephone: 1-800-221-4268.

Rebalancing Your Portfolio

Do you need to constantly rebalance your mutual fund portfolio? Is rebalancing a constructive strategy for fine-tuning or is it needless and possibly harmful tinkering? Our Benchmark Master Model Portfolio already adjusts asset allocation every six years. Is it needed more often?

Our rebalancing schedule reflects the reality that most people need to alter their risk/reward profile as they progress from their early earning years when they can take the most risk, to retirement when income and safety are paramount. While that progression is very orderly, it doesn't account for the fact that markets don't march in straight, predetermined lines. Large market moves can knock the tidy sequence out of whack. If, for instance, international stocks soar compared to U.S. large-cap stocks, as happened in 1993 (T. Rowe Price International gained 40.1%, while Vanguard Index 500 returned 9.9%), should you trim back the international stock allocation and add to lagging large-cap U.S. stocks? How important is it to get back to the original allocation percentages? And how often?

As a case example, let's see what market fluctuation did to the portfolio of our 38-year-old investor the first year:

	One-Year Change			
	Original Portfolio January 1, 1993	%	Portfolio After Market Fluctuation January 1, 1994	%
U.S. Treasuries	$15,000	(30)	$16,483	(28)
Vanguard Index 500	21,000	(42)	23,076	(39)
Vanguard Index Small-Cap	3,500	(7)	4,154	(7)
T. Rowe Price Small-Cap*	3,500	(7)	4,315	(7)
T. Rowe Price International	7,000	(14)	9,808	(17)
Total	$50,000	(100%)	$57,836	(100%)

*T. Rowe Price Small-Cap Value Fund was still available during the period shown.

Not very dramatic, is it? Let's look at the change after three years:

		Three-Year Change		
	Original Portfolio *January 1, 1993*		*Portfolio After* *Market* *Fluctuation* *January 1, 1996*	
		%		%
U.S. Treasuries	$15,000	(30)	$18,686	(26)
Vanguard Index 500	21,000	(42)	32,093	(44)
Vanguard Index Small-Cap	3,500	(7)	5,321	(7)
T. Rowe Price Small-Cap	3,500	(7)	5,502	(8)
T. Rowe Price International	7,000	(14)	10,841	(15)
Total	$50,000	(100%)	$72,443	(100%)

Percentage allocations were still not dramatically changed. However, for the sake of illustration, we'll rebalance assets back to the original percentages. An important proviso is that we do this within the stock allocations only because we feel that rebalancing the total portfolio will constantly reduce the winning asset allocation (stocks) to nonwinning (bonds) prematurely, like cutting back weeds to let flowers grow.

Stock Fund-Only Rebalancing

Total portfolio value	$72,443
Minus U.S. Treasuries value	18,686
Stock funds to be reallocated	$53,757

To rebalance, calculate the percentages *within* the stock fund category only, from the original portfolio:

Original Portfolio

		Portfolio Percentage	Stock Funds Percentage
U.S. Treasuries	$15,000	30%	
Vanguard Index 500	21,000	42	60%
Vanguard Index Small-Cap	3,500	7	10
T. Rowe Price Small-Cap	3,500	7	10
T. Rowe Price International	7,000	14	<u>20</u>
	<u>35,000</u>		
Totals	$50,000	100%	100%

Rebalance the stock funds ($53,757), using the original portfolio's percentage allocations:

Rebalanced (Stock Funds Only) Portfolio

		Portfolio Percentage	Stock Funds Percentage
U.S. Treasuries	$18,686	26%	
Vanguard Index 500	32,254	44	60%
Vanguard Index Small-Cap	5,376	7	10
T. Rowe Price Small-Cap	5,376	7	10
T. Rowe Price International	<u>10,751</u>	15	20
	$53,757	100%*	100%
Totals	$72,443		

*Doesn't total 100% due to rounding.

Obviously, the differences between the portfolio before and after rebalancing are so minor in this example that they were hardly worth figuring. Since most funds impose $500 or $1,000 minimums for these kind of transactions, you couldn't have rebalanced anyway. Doing the math, however, would have shown you were still essentially "on track."

Should You Rebalance?

A whole cottage industry of professional rebalancers—
investment advisors and financial planners—has sprung
up using elaborate computer programs that create opti-
mization analyses, expected rates of return, correlation
coefficients, factor models, and the like, all designed to
solve your rebalancing "problems." However, if anybody
has a problem, it is probably the pros. If their customers
have graduated to index funds, rebalancing is the only
service left for which professionals can still charge fees.
Although many talk loud and long about the merits of rebalancing, don't take it too seriously and, most of all,
don't overpay for the rebalancing services. Our feeling is
that, as a rule, you should rebalance only very occasionally, particularly if there are no major changes in the
value of your funds.

   If you are looking for the highest very long-term returns, we recommend against rebalancing for several
reasons:

* Markets tend to rebalance themselves.
* You create tax liabilities if you are investing taxable
  dollars.
* You transfer your stake from asset classes with the
  highest returns to those with lower returns.
* This goes against the successful long-term strategy
  of letting your profits run (and compound).

   Like most investors, perhaps, your horizons are considerably shorter than the very long term. If so, periodic rebalancing may not be a bad idea because, compared to
other more damaging strategies, it is relatively harmless,
particularly if it makes you feel better to visit your money
every once in a while.

   Done sensibly, rebalancing accomplishes the following:

* It keeps you on track with your original game plan. If the plan was good enough to make up in the first place, unless your circumstances change, it ought to be good enough to stick with.
* It can help avoid the short-to-intermediate problem of what brokers call "whiplash"—short-term investors' proclivity to buy high and sell low. If you are a closet trader, rebalancing gives you something to tinker with and a chance to hum the Wall Street Lullaby ("Buy low, sell high") correctly instead of usually getting it backward.
* Rebalancing can dampen portfolio volatility because not all asset classes go in the same direction at the same time. This becomes more and more important as retirement approaches or becomes a reality.

Over intermediate-term cycles, taking advantage of the markets' fads and fancies may be rewarding. In an article titled, "Worst to First," *Morningstar*'s John Rekenthaler (April 4, 1994) showed very successful results in one period from investing in asset classes with no other criterion than that they had the worst five-year returns. As it turned out, the "worst" assets delivered the best returns over the following five years and the "best" delivered the worst results.

Reversing Field

Objective	1989 5-Year Results*	1994 5-Year Results*	
(1) International stock	20.60%	9.37%	(6)
(2) Equity-income	14.31	11.21	(5)
(3) Growth and income	14.20	11.90	(4)
(4) Growth	13.30	13.90	(3)
(5) Small company	10.26	15.87	(2)
(6) Aggressive growth	8.91	16.13	(1)

*Trailing five-year returns through February 28, 1989 and February 28, 1994.

What were investors actually doing at the time? You guessed it: Morningstar's accompanying table (not shown) also revealed that investors were doing precisely the opposite: funneling more money into the "best" asset classes and the least amount of money into the "worst."

Rekenthaler observed, "Time would show, though, that they had it all backward. In the succeeding five years, diversified stock funds have exactly reversed their previous order. *Rather than purchasing what had worked, aspiring investors would have been better off loading up on funds from the worst-performing objective and skipping those of the best*" [emphasis added].*

We aren't making a table-pounding case for rebalancing. It can be helpful in reducing volatility, it gives market meddlers something to do, and it offers a discipline which makes more sense than most, if only because it makes you go in the opposite direction of the crowd. And in those instances where it may convert incurable market timers to long-term investors, rebalancing might be truly significant.

Autopilot Investing

A fanatic is someone who can't change his mind and won't change the subject.

Winston Churchill

As enthusiastic as we are about indexing, we stop well short of recommending that you index every last investable dime, that is, putting the portfolio on autopilot. While constant tinkering is usually harmful, a Rip Van Winkle investment strategy takes benign neglect to the extreme. Further, it's hard not to harbor some reservations about a "one-shoe-fits-all" approach, particularly one in the no-brainer category.

*Morningstar Mutual Funds, Morningstar, Inc., Chicago, Illinois, 800-876-5005.

Nevertheless, it is hard to argue intellectually against a 100% indexed portfolio; it simply takes indexing to the ultimate. After all, if it has proven to be so effective in efficient markets, and all markets seem to be getting more efficient, why fight it? Isn't indexing the whole portfolio *the* most logical approach? We don't think so, even though the only cerebral argument we can muster is the old saw, "if it seems too good to be true, it probably is."

Are we indexing enthusiasts, advocates, purists, or zealots? At this point, we fancy ourselves as advocates. You have to find your rightful place on the scale. Of one thing we are certain: Wall Street is murky enough. The last thing we want to do is leave you in a fog of semantics.

So here is the purist's delight: a totally indexed womb-to-tomb mutual fund portfolio. Using our Benchmark Asset Allocation Model and our theoretical 38-year-old's $50,000 portfolio, here are the recommended funds:

Autopilot Model Portfolio

	Bonds—30%
$7,500	Vanguard Short-Term Bond Portfolio
7,500	Vanguard Intermediate-Term Portfolio
15,000	
	Large-Cap Stocks—42%
$21,000	Vanguard Index Trust 500 Portfolio
	Small-Cap Stocks—14%
$7,000	Vanguard Index Small-Cap Fund
	International Stocks—14%
$7,000	Vanguard Total International Portfolio

Note: The autopilot model portfolio, containing nothing but Vanguard Index Funds, may seem like a thinly disguised Vanguard infomercial. In the interest of diversity, we searched for other index funds to recommend, but kept running into the same comparative costs problem: Typically, other funds' costs were 0.25% to 0.75% more per annum. So, at the risk of giving the false impression that we're Vanguard groupies, we decided to stick with Vanguard—the lowest-cost provider.

If you decide to put your portfolio on autopilot, there is an additional benefit: It is virtually maintenance-free. To reallocate in keeping with our asset allocation progression, you need only rise from your recliner and make one phone call every six years. It's a toll-free number at that.

7

The Index Fund Universe

A comparison or ranking of index funds, with so many having such short histories, has to focus on costs. Once you have identified the asset classes to invest in, the next step is to find the funds with the lowest costs within that class. The rationale is that since an index fund's only mission is to track its target index, then the lower its costs, the closer it should get to delivering index-like returns. Differences, such as size efficiency and other factors, may prove to be important, but experience is too limited to know whether to measure them. Until proven otherwise, the subject of costs is the best place to start.

Before we go to the line-up, you should know about several types of index funds:

* Exchange-listed index funds
* Turbocharged funds
* Dimensional Fund Advisors (DFA)

Exchange-Listed Index Funds

Don't be so humble, you're not that great.

Golda Meir

Not to be outdone by index funds, both the American and New York Stock Exchange have come up with versions of

their own. Index funds are good for their members because
their retail brokers can finally offer indexing to their customers—and charge commissions. It might even be good
for index investors because the main advantage of exchange-listed index funds is their immediate liquidity—
broker-speak for the fact that they can be bought and sold
on the exchange within minutes. However, liquidity can
also be a two-edged sword, turning index fund investors
into index fund traders, but we've preached our last on the
subject.

Technically, listed funds are *unit trusts,* which are unmanaged portfolios of full proportionate shares of stocks
that are held by a custodian (usually a bank) and that
mimic their target index. Like open-end index funds, they
can expand and contract asset size to fit the number of investors. How they do so is a bit technical, but here is what
is important:

* Unlike open-end funds, redeeming shareholders cannot force the fund to sell portfolio shares because they sell
their shares on the exchanges rather than back to the fund.
It remains to be seen whether a redemption logjam in open-
end funds might occur during turbulent market conditions
in open-end funds (Chapter 3). If a logjam developed, listed index shares could have an advantage.

* Unlike listed closed-end trusts, listed index shares
don't drop to deep discounts (or rise to premiums) to NAV
because of the activity of arbitrageurs ("arbs"). Arbs are
professional traders who continually profit from small
price disparities, which keep the price of listed index
shares extremely close to their target index during trading
hours. According to the American Stock Exchange, historical correlation between NAV and price has been very close.
In essence, arbs keep the market for listed index shares extremely efficient.

* Most open-end index funds redeem shares by telephone up to the markets' closing—at that day's closing price—and automatically mail a check for the proceeds the next day. Before reinvesting, you have to wait for the check's arrival and then mail it to its next worthy destination. Wiring reinvestment funds can speed things up, but it's still awkward if you're in a hurry. With listed index funds, if hair trigger turnaround is important, you can turn around as often as you want—many times a day, rather than just once at closing prices. If that's your persuasion, listed funds are a better choice. Remember, though, that indexing, like a skin blemish, is best left alone.

Compared to open-end index funds, listed index funds are in their infancy. The first "Spiders" (Standard & Poor's Depository Receipts, or SPDRs) targeted the S&P 500 and began trading on the American Stock Exchange in 1993. More recently, the S&P Mid-Cap 400 was introduced. Annual expense ratios are modest: 0.185% for the 500 and 0.30% for the 400.

In 1996, the AMEX introduced WEBS, World Equity Benchmark Shares. WEBS index series are single-county index funds that target the Morgan Stanley Capital International (MSCI) Indexes for 17 foreign countries:

Australia	Malaysia
Austria	Mexico
Belgium	Netherlands
Canada	Singapore
France	Spain
Germany	Sweden
Hong Kong	Switzerland
Italy	United Kingdom
Japan	

Total annual operating costs for WEBS are estimated to be 0.80%, about half that of the average managed fund, but considerably more than many of the international index funds.

Not to be outdone, the New York Stock Exchange introduced single-country listed index shares in 1996. Called CountryBaskets, they track the Financial Times/Standard & Poor's country indexes of nine foreign stock markets and project an "all-inclusive" (annual) cost ratio of 0.84%. CountryBasket shares represent stock markets in:

Australia	Japan
France	South Africa
Germany	United Kingdom
Hong Kong	United States
Italy	

Exhibit 7-1 is an exchange-listed index fund directory. If you would like to receive information on these funds, call the American Stock Exchange at 1-800-THE-AMEX and the New York Stock Exchange at 1-888-8CB-INFO.

Exhibit 7-1 Exchange-listed index fund directory.

Fund	Exchange Symbol	Index	Expense Ratio %
SPDR 500	ASE/SPY	S&P 500	0.185
S&P Mid-Cap	ASE/MDY	S&P 400 Mid-Cap Index	0.30
World Equity Benchmark Shares (WEBS)			
WEBS Australia	ASE/EWA	MSCI Australia	0.80e*
WEBS Austria	ASE/EWO	MSCI Austria	
WEBS Belgium	ASE/EWK	MSCI Belgium	
WEBS Canada	ASE/EWC	MSCI Canada	
WEBS France	ASE/EWQ	MSCI France	

WEBS Germany	ASE/EWG	MSCI Germany	
WEBS Hong Kong	ASE/EWH	MSCI Hong Kong	
WEBS Italy	ASE/EWI	MSCI Italy	
WEBS Japan	ASE/EWJ	MSCI Japan	
WEBS Malaysia	ASE/EWM	MSCI Malaysia	
WEBS Mexico	ASE/EWW	MSCI Mexico	
WEBS Netherlands	ASE/EWN	MSCI Netherlands	
WEBS Singapore	ASE/EWS	MSCI Singapore	
WEBS Spain	ASE/EWP	MSCI Spain	
WEBS Sweden	ASE/EWD	MSCI Sweden	
WEBS Switzerland	ASE/EWL	MSCI Switzerland	
WEBS United Kingdom	ASE/EWU	MSCI United Kingdom	

CountryBaskets

CB Australia	NYSE/GXA	Finl Times/S&P Australia	0.84e**
CB France	NYSE/GXF	Finl Times/S&P France	
CB Germany	NYSE/GXG	Finl Time/S&P Germany	
CB Hong Kong	NYSE/GXH	Finl Times/S&P Hong Kong	
CB Italy	NYSE/GXI	Finl Times/S&P Italy	
CB Japan	NYSE/GXJ	Finl Times/S&P Japan	
CB South Africa	NYSE/GXR	Finl Times/S&P South Africa	
CB United Kingdom	NYSE/GXK	Finl Times/S&P United Kingdom	
CB United States	NYSE/GXU	Finl Times/S&P United States	

*All WEBS have an estimated expense ratio of 0.80%.
**All CountryBaskets have an estimated 0.84% expense ratio (e = estimated).

Turbocharged Index Funds

Always walk, never run. Runnin' jangles up the juices.

Satchel Paige

It's not always easy to leave well enough alone, particularly when you don't get paid much for it, and so many folks are doing the same thing.

So it is not surprising that a number of "enhanced" index funds should appear. The common objective is to do the index one better, although the techniques vary. Some funds use "black boxes" (computer-based trading systems), some use derivatives, and some use options.

Money magazine (August 1995) found that eight so-called index funds tracked by *Morningstar* have trailed the S&P 500 over the past 5 years: 9.37% versus 11.41%. Our own research found that, within the small universe of enhancers, a number have given up.

Since only one in four or five managed funds beat index funds, it was no surprise that the odds were not much different with the quasi-index funds: Out of the nine enhancers that we uncovered, three emerged as qualified winners. We say "qualified" because the evidence is too limited to be totally convincing. Another concern is that index-enhancing funds may simply be taking more risk than their target index, and the next bear market may take back all the enhanced returns and then some.

A brief description of the three qualified no-load quasi-index "winners" follows:

* *Fidelity Disciplined Equity.* Managed with an artificial intelligence (sometimes called neural networking) "black box." Disciplined Equity's mandate is to generate higher returns than the S&P 500. In the six years from 1989 through 1994, it roared ahead of the index by an average annual margin of 3.95%. In 1995, however, technology stocks hit the wall, and the fund lagged the index by a whopping 8.52%.

Even so, five-year average annual returns were 18.45% versus the S&P 500's 16.58%. Portfolio manager Brad Lewis seems to be continually changing the software he is using in an attempt to keep ahead of the index. Whether the constant fine-tuning will allow the fund to stay ahead of the pack or drop back remains to be seen. Considering 1995's disappointing results and the fact that the fund's brakes have not been tested in a bear market, we would not bet the farm on Fidelity Disciplined Equity.

* *Smith Breeden Market Tracking Fund.* Despite its tiny size—$5 million—it sports Bill Sharpe, winner of the 1990 Nobel Prize in Economic Sciences, on its supervising Board of Directors, along with a three-year history of beating the S&P 500 by between 1 and 2% annually, depending on the time period measured. Smith Breeden invests 95% of the fund in short-term mortgage bonds and the remaining 5% in S&P futures contracts. The efficiency of investing in futures instead of directly in S&P stocks and the returns gained from the mortgage bond portfolio have produced index-beating results. This fund does not offer the tax advantages of most index funds (Chapter 3). So using it in a tax-deferred qualified plan is most appropriate. Smith Breeden's strategy has yet to be tested by a bear market in either stocks or bonds. Until it is, there is no way to know whether its enhancing strategy, which has done so well so far, will hold up.

* *Vanguard Quantitative.* It has beaten the S&P 500 in six out of ten years. For the five years ending December 31, 1995, it returned 16.48% annually, trailing the S&P 500's return of 16.58%, but beating the sister Vanguard Index 500 by an infinitesimal 0.07% annually. If you're wondering why you should bother, apparently so has management. They are tweaking the computer modeling to allow a slightly higher risk/reward profile. In a bull market, this fund may do a sliver better than the Vanguard Index 500, but not for taxable investment dollars. Portfolio turnover has been much higher with the resultant tax consequences.

One of the attractions of index funds is predictability; whether the asset class does well or badly, you're pretty sure to "get yours." So it is hard to get worked up about enhanced index funds that interfere with this assurance. Also, the trade-off seems to be the same as with managed funds: poor odds that you'll beat the index to start with, and worse odds that you can pick the future winners that will beat the index significantly. Further, none have been through really adverse market conditions. These and other quasi-index funds appear in the Index Fund Directory (Chapter 8) with "Enhanced" appearing after the index description.

DFA—State-of-the-Art Indexing

How do I work? I grope.

Albert Einstein

Most people associate indexing with the Vanguard fund family and think of their chairman, John Bogle, as the father of indexing.

Yet another important index fund management company deserves attention: Dimensional Fund Advisors (DFA). DFA's Chairman, Rex Sinquefield, launched the first index fund, an institutional S&P 500 index fund, in 1973. Founded to serve institutional clients in 1981, they oversee private and mutual fund assets of over $15 billion.

DFA, besides tending to the billions under management, is also a sort of leading edge think tank. Its stable of mutual funds invests in just about any asset class conceivable. There is an international fund that invests only in small-cap stocks, one that invests in small-cap stocks on the European continent, in the United Kingdom, or Japan, or one that invests in large-cap U.S. value or in small-cap U.S. value. Their selection should satisfy the most ardent indexing purist.

In addition, they have reams of data showing historical returns and risks of just about any asset class or asset class mix imaginable over the last 20 years. What distinguishes DFA's stable of funds from most others is that they offer only funds where academic research has shown "sweet spots": asset classes that have shown sufficient rewards for the risks taken. They reject offering funds of asset classes whose historical reward/risk returns have not been salubrious, such as long-term bond funds.

DFA's obscurity stems from the fact that they don't do business directly with the public. And they aren't being coy; their specialty is money management, not marketing. They are the only fund management company on the planet without a toll-free number. There are good reasons for DFA's reluctance: Promoting retail business is costly, and as we know, all too often retail "investors" become traders.

Another reason for their skittishness is that they need to protect some of their small-cap specialized funds, which they characterize as "fragile to participant behavior," from sudden heavy redemptions. If a run occurred, the fund would have to sell relatively illiquid stocks quickly and be adversely affected by wide market spreads and high transaction costs.

The only way you can invest in these funds is through a small cadre of registered investment advisors (approximately 300), who DFA feels are knowledgeable, index-savvy, and in touch with DFA funds—and who will use a long-term investment strategy.

That's the good news. The bad news is that DFA doesn't make the list of the anointed available, and the discount brokers we called to ferret out DFA-approved advisors weren't entirely helpful. One brokerage firm grudgingly provided the name of one advisor; another suggested we visit the library.

If you're intrigued and happen on a DFA-approved advisor who can channel you into DFA funds, we have only two caveats:

* Don't get carried away by the lure of state-of-the-art index sophistication and pay too much in advisor fees because you'll lose one of indexing's main advantages: low costs.

* Even though DFA's historical asset class research was pioneering and innovative, the past provides only guidelines—not even near guarantees of future returns. What is guaranteed is that DFA has done more historical indexing homework than most and is totally committed to its disciplines. The part that is not guaranteed is, of course, which asset classes will be future winners.

Note: Since DFA's funds are not available directly, we did not include them in our Index Fund Directory.

Paying a Sales Load—If You Must

God gives us our relatives; thank God we can choose our friends.

Ethel Mumford

By now we are far beyond any question about paying a sales load. Yet sometimes life serves up less than ideal circumstances that call for innovation and compromise, and in some instances the consequences of escaping the load or commissions are worse than paying them. As difficult as it is for us no-load indexing advocates to admit, in a few instances, you're better off paying the fees. For example:

* What if you have a close personal relationship with your broker who is your daughter-in-law, former college roommate, or your next-door neighbor, and who has become a close friend? Forget what the books say: You cannot "take money away" and not destroy your friendship.

The problem, however, doesn't go away because the law of averages is massively indifferent to loyalty and friendship. Since full-service brokers, as high-cost providers, fight unforgiving odds, your returns have probably been below average. While closing your account and dispatching a check to the index funds might be the quickest fix to your investment problem, obviously the fix would create other problems.

* Another common situation arises from the fact that millions of advertising dollars have convinced you that, without talking to serious folks (wearing suits) in an appropriate setting (the dignified bustle of a brokerage office), the investment process is somehow incomplete. When you "invest" at the bank, you don't roll over your CDs standing in the rain at an ATM machine. You're warm and comfortably seated on the other side of a desk from a friendly "savings specialist" (not just a teller), who explains things. You may feel that mutual fund investing, which is more complex, deserves no less; that if you don't get the treatment you and your important money deserve, you'll just leave it in the bank where they "treat you right."

* In contrast, speaking on the phone with faceless, sometimes indifferent fund marketers and then mailing a check while you're still in your bathrobe may seem like a last-class way to invest for first-class returns. Even if you can get past the mental block of investing while wearing your jammies, you may still think that somebody has to be minding the store at the fund. If indexing seems like handing your fate over to a computer nerd mindlessly chasing indexes, we have the solution: a load-fund family recommended at the end of this section. An added bonus is that it comes with a broker wearing a suit.

* Perhaps you're acting in the capacity of trustee, pension fund administrator, guardian, or other fiduciary position, responsible for overseeing investments (or at least handling paperwork) for others. This is usually a less than salubrious situation because you and the "others" often have no investment experience.

These problems are not solved simply by ponying up sales loads or commissions. The solution is to make the best choices among the mind-boggling number of alternatives—and trying to get at least some of your money's worth from the commissions and fees. Most of all, you want to make sure that your fees are not buying merchandise riddled with conflicts of interest that only cause more problems.

If your problem is "taking money away" from a valued friend or relative, a simple and very satisfactory solution can be found in exchange-listed SPDRs (Spiders) or S&P Mid-Cap 400 shares (Chapter 7). They sport very low expense ratios and provide all the indexing perks (except automatic dividend reinvestment) as open-end index funds and a touch more liquidity. How do they save your friendship? They are bought through your broker. These funds solve most of your problem if you're disposed to indexing your entire portfolio. One caution: Don't get sidetracked into mainstream, load-charging, open-end index funds because, in addition to imposing a sales charge, they also include higher annual expenses.

If your problem is dignifying the investment process, the solution might be investing, through earnest and conservatively dressed brokers, in exchange-listed index funds or our recommended managed open-end fund family that charges a sales load. Because both generate commissions, someone will be delighted to sit down with you and treat you right.

But if you are a fiduciary or administrator, your only choice is a load-charging, open-end fund family. You do not want to explain indexing or SPDRs to trust beneficiaries or pension fund participants, whose attention spans are unlikely to go the distance. With a load fund, you have an important ally: the fund sales representative from the distributor or brokerage house. Also, at least to get everybody started, you can often count on significant assistance from a fund family representative, called a *wholesaler*. They can sort out technicalities, expedite paperwork, and, most importantly, explain investment options to those who need it most. On an ongoing basis, part of their job is also handholding, so that you don't have to answer questions about why the market went up or down. You pass them on to the professionals who are in the business of providing ready explanations. In addition, they—not you—can be responsible for providing guidance on that critical issue: asset allocation.

Our Recommendation

Our recommendation for an open-end load fund family is Capital Research and Management, sometimes better known as The American Funds. You may not be familiar with them because, unlike their competition, they don't plaster mountain charts and Morningstar rankings (good as they are) all over the landscape. They hardly advertise at all. Despite their public silence, they are a thundering presence in the mutual fund industry, managing over $160 billion in 28 funds, making them the third largest in the business.

While their funds show up only occasionally in the hottest-funds-of-the-quarter tables, over the longer term, they more than make up for it with consistent performance.

There are a number of reasons: Underlying it all is Capital Research's corporate culture. There are no "star" portfolio managers. Each fund is run with a multiple manager structure. Important managers and analysts are paid (very) well and own a piece of the privately held company; management turnover is low. Despite their Los Angeles location, where some might hold meetings while roller blading, they run money the old-fashioned way: as long-term investors. American's funds typically hold stocks for five years in an industry in which even a two-year holding period is considered geriatric.

Their corporate culture shines through in another way: Compared to much of their competition, there is no question that investors share in the pie. There is no tangled terrain of share classes with by-gas-chamber-or-by-hanging "choices." American Funds come in only one flavor: up-front loads with maximums ranging between 4.75% and 5.75%. And annual expense ratios are only about half of the industry's.

American has also distinguished itself by its refusal to bring out trendy funds just because investors clamored for them. By avoiding fads, they have spared themselves considerable embarrassment and saved their shareholders substantial sums of money.

Is the picture perfect? It never is. There is always the risk that management sells out to a buyer determined to exploit the spread between American's fees and the industry average. Boosting costs to "just" the industry average would increase management's annual take (and reduce shareholder returns) by close to $1 billion annually.

But let's not borrow trouble. Sixty years of tradition are woven into the corporate culture, and they may stay the course for yet another 60. If paying a sales load is a "must," our pick for the best buy is the American Funds family. Telephone: 1-800-421-4120.

Index Funds—Lining Them Up

A conclusion is the place where you get tired of thinking.

Martin Fisher

We can "rank" index funds, but the rankings have no correlation to returns unless comparable funds are tracking the same index.

We have divided index funds into five categories:

* U.S. stock funds
* Bond funds
* Flexible portfolio (stocks and bonds)
* International stock funds
* International single-country stock funds

The rankings that follow are inverse to costs; that is, the lower the costs, the higher the ranking. It remains to be seen whether managements with equal costs are more skillful tracking a particular index than others. Variations in returns, however, should not prove to be as large as the differences between managed funds with the same objective.

Maximum sales loads are shown, but are not considered in the rankings because they vary depending on:

* The amount invested.
* Whether they are front- or back-end loaded.
* The investment period.

Some funds charging redemption fees impose them only during the first year or sooner. Because the fees are constantly changed, check the current expenses and load charges of funds you are considering.

Funds attempting to provide returns that exceed their target index or that lower its risk profile are shown as "enhanced." Both exchange-listed and open-end funds are included. Exchange-listed index funds are bought or sold through brokers whose commission can be negotiated, so we list "Neg." in the sales load column. Telephone numbers of all funds are shown in the Index Fund Directory in Chapter 8.

U.S. Stock Index Fund Rankings

Fund	Expense Ratio	Objective	Index	Sales Load
USAA S&P 500 Index Fund	0.18	Growth & Income	S&P 500	None
SPDR 500 (Listed ASE)	0.185	Growth & Income	S&P 500	Neg.
Seven Seas S&P 500	0.19	Growth & Income	S&P 500	None
Vanguard Index 500 Port.	0.19	Growth & Income	S&P 500	None
Calif. Trust II S&P 500	0.20	Growth & Income	S&P 500	None
Dreyfus Inst. S&P 500	0.20	Growth & Income	S&P 500	None
MasterWorks S&P Stock Fund	0.20	Growth & Income	S&P 500	None
Vanguard Index Extended Market	0.20	Mid-Cap	Wilshire 4500	None
Vanguard Index Growth Port.	0.20	Growth	S&P/BARRA Growth Index	None
Vanguard Index Value Port.	0.20	Growth & Income	S&P BARRA Value Index	None
Vanguard Tax-Managed Capital Appreciation	0.20	Growth	Russell 1000	2.00
Vanguard Tax-Managed Growth & Income	0.20	Growth & Income	S&P 500	2.00
Vanguard Total Stock Market Portfolio	0.20	Growth	Wilshire 5000	None

e = estimated
* = no valid comparisons with other funds because of expense structure

Fund	Expense Ratio	Objective	Index	Sales Load
BT Pyramid: Inv. Equity 500	0.25	Growth & Income	S&P 500	None
SEI Index S&P 500	0.25	Growth & Income	S&P 500	None
Vanguard Index Small-Cap Portfolio	0.25	Small Company Growth	Russell 2000	1.00
Schwab S&P 500 eShares	0.28	Growth & Income	S&P 500	None
Federated Max-Cap	0.29	Growth & Income	S&P 500	None
S&P Mid-Cap (Listed ASE)	0.30	Growth	S&P 400 Mid-Cap Index	Neg.
Munder Index 500 A	0.35	Growth & Income	S&P 500	None
Nations Equity Index Trust A	0.35	Growth & Income	S&P 500	None
Vanguard Real Estate Index	0.35e	Real Est	MSCI REIT Index	1.00
Corefund Equity Index A	0.37	Growth & Income	S&P 500	None
Galaxy II Large Company Index	0.38	Growth & Income	S&P 500	None
Calif Trust II	0.40	Growth	S&P 400	None
Dreyfus S&P 500	0.40	Growth	S&P 500	None
Galaxy II Small Co Index	0.40	Small Company Growth	Russell 2000	None
Galaxy II Utility Index	0.40	Utility	Russell 1000 Utility Subset	None

e = estimated
* = no valid comparisons with other funds because of expense structure

Fund	Expense Ratio	Objective	Index	Sales Load
Woodward Equity Index	0.41	Growth & Income	S&P 500	None
Fidelity Market Index	0.45	Growth & Income	S&P 500	None
Harris Insight Index Fund CL C	0.45	Growth & Income	S&P 500	None
T. Rowe Price Index: Equity	0.45	Growth & Income	S&P 500	None
Jackson National Growth	0.46	Growth & Income	S&P 500	4.75
Vanguard Quantitative	0.48	Growth & Income	S&P 500 Enhanced	None
Schwab S&P 500 Investor Shares	0.49	Growth & Income	S&P 500	None
Dreyfus Mid-Cap Index	0.50	Growth	S&P 400	None
Norwest Advantage Index Fund	0.50	Growth & Income	S&P 500	None
Schwab 1000	0.54	Growth & Income	1,000 largest U.S. corporations	0.50
Dreyfus S&P 500	0.55	Growth & Income	S&P 500	None
One Group Equity Index A	0.56	Growth & Income	S&P 500	4.50
First American Equity Index A	0.57	Growth & Income	S&P 500	4.50
Victory Stock Index	0.58	Growth & Income	S&P 500	4.75
Federated Mid-Cap	0.60	Mid-Cap	S&P 400	None

e = estimated
* = no valid comparisons with other funds because of expense structure

Fund	Expense Ratio	Objective	Index	Sales Load
Kent Funds Equity Index	0.60	Growth & Income	S&P 500	4.00
Compass Cap Idx. Equity Port. A	0.65	Growth & Income	S&P 500	3.00
Wilshire Target Small Company Value	0.66	Small Company Growth	Wilsh. 5000 Sm. Co. Val. Subset	None
Schwab Small-Cap Index	0.67	Small Company Growth	Schwab Small-Cap Index	0.50
Seven Seas Matrix Equity	0.68	Growth	S&P 500 Enhanced	None
Harris Insight Index Fund CL A	0.70	Growth & Income	S&P 500	4.50
Munder Index 500 B	0.70	Growth & Income	S&P 500	None
United Services All Amer. Equity	0.70	Growth	S&P 500 Enhanced	None
Portico Equity Index	0.72	Growth & Income	S&P 500	4.00
Federated Mini-Cap	0.74	Small Company Growth	Russell 2000	None
ASM	0.75	Growth & Income	Dow Jones 30 Industrials	None
Transamerica Premier Index	0.75	Growth & Income	S&P 500	None
Wilshire Target Large Company Value	0.77	Growth	Wilsh. 5000 Lg. Co. Val. Subset	None

e = estimated
* = no valid comparisons with other funds because of expense structure

Fund	Expense Ratio	Objective	Index	Sales Load
Principal Pres. PSE Tech. Index	0.80	Specialty	Pac. Stk. Exch. Tech. Index	4.50
Wilshire Target Company Growth	0.80	Growth	Wilsh. 5000 Lg. Co. Gr. Subset	None
CountryBasket United States	0.84e	Growth & Income	Finl. Times/ S&P United States	Neg.
Rushmore Amer. Gas Index	0.85	Natural Resources	American Gas Association Stock Index	None
Biltmore Equity	0.87	Growth & Income	S&P 500	4.50
Domini Social Equity	0.90*	Growth	400 Co. Index Social Criteria	None
Mainstay Equity	0.90	Growth & Income	S&P 500	3.00
Smith Breeden Market Tracking	0.90	Growth	S&P 500 Enhanced	None
Wilshire Target Small Company Growth	0.91	Small Company Growth	Wilsh. 5000 Small Company Growth Subset	None
Stagecoach Corp. Stock	0.96	Growth & Income	S&P 500	None
Weiss Peck & Greer Quantitative Equity	1.14	Growth	S&P 500 Enhanced	None
Principal Pres. S&P 100	1.20	Growth & Income	S&P 100 Enhanced	4.50

e = estimated
* = no valid comparisons with other funds because of expense structure

Fund	Expense Ratio	Objective	Index	Sales Load
Gateway Index Plus	1.21	Growth	S&P 100 Enhanced	None
One Group Equity Index B	1.31	Growth & Income	S&P 500	5.00
First Amer. Equity Index B	1.35	Growth & Income	S&P 500	5.00
Compass Cap Index Equity Portfolio B	1.40	Growth & Income	S&P 500	4.50
Colonial Small Stock A	1.45	Small Company Growth	Smallest 1/5 Cap NYSE	5.75
Dean Witter Value Added Equity	1.64	Growth	S&P 500 Enhanced	5.00
Gateway Small-Cap Index	2.00	Small Company Growth	Wilshire Small-Cap Index 90%	None
Colonial Small Stock B	2.20	Small Company Growth	Smallest 1/5 Cap NYSE	5.00
Bhirud Mid-Cap Growth	2.68	Mid-Cap	S&P 400 Enhanced	5.75
Atlanta Growth	6.49	Atlanta Companies	Specialty	3.75

Bond Index Fund Rankings

Fund	Expense Ratio	Objective	Index	Sales Load
Vanguard Intermediate-Term Bond Portfolio	0.18	Fixed Income Intermediate Term	Lehman 5–10 Government Corp. Bd. Index	None

e = estimated
* = no valid comparisons with other funds because of expense structure

Fund	Expense Ratio	Objective	Index	Sales Load
Vanguard Short-Term Bond Portfolio	0.18	Fixed Income Short-Term	Lehman 1–3 Gvt./Corp. Bond Index	None
Vanguard Long-Term Bond Portfolio	0.20	Fixed Income Long-Term	Lehman 20–25 Gvt./Corp. Bond Index	None
MasterWorks Bond Index	0.23	Fixed Income Long-Term	Lehman Gvt. Corp. Bd. Index	None
Federated Bond Index	0.29	Fixed Income	Lehman Aggreg. Bond Index	None
Fidelity U.S. Bond Index	0.32	Fixed Income	Lehman Aggreg. Bond Index	None
SEI Index Bond	0.38	Fixed Income	Salomon Broad Inv. Grade Bond Index	None
Galaxy II Treasury Index	0.40	Fixed Income	Salomon Inv. Grade Bond Index	None
Dreyfus Bond Market Index	0.65	Fixed Income	Lehman Government/ Corporate Bond Index	None
Portico Bond IMMEDX	0.70	Fixed Income	Lehman Investment Government Corporate Bond Index	2.00

e = estimated
* = no valid comparisons with other funds because of expense structure

Fund	Expense Ratio	Objective	Index	Sales Load
Smith Breeden Intermediate-Duration U.S. Government	0.70	Fixed Income Enhanced	Salomon Mortgage Index	None
Smith Breeden Short-Duration U.S. Government	0.70	Fixed Income	U.S. Treas. 6-mo. Enhanced	None
Portico Interm Bond Market	0.75	Fixed Income Intermedi-ate Term	Lehman 5–10 Government Corporate Bond Index	2.00
Portico Short-Term Bond Mkt.	0.75	Fixed Income Short Term	Lehman 1–3 Gvt. Corp. Bond Index	2.00

Flexible Portfolio Index Fund Rankings

Fund	Expense Ratio	Objective	Index	Sales Load
Vanguard Bal. Index	0.20	Flexible	Wilshire 5000/ Salomon Investment Grade Bond Index	None
Vanguard Tax-Mgd. Balanced	0.20	Flexible	Russell 1000/ Managed Muni Bonds	2.00
MasterWorks Funds		Flexible Enhanced	Index Segments of	
LifePath 2000	0.95		17 global	None
LifePath 2010	0.95		equity &	None
LifePath 2020	0.95		debt markets	None
LifePath 2030	0.95			None
LifePath 2040	0.95			None

e = estimated
* = no valid comparisons with other funds because of expense structure

Fund	Expense Ratio	Objective	Index	Sales Load
Stagecoach:				
Lifepath 2000	1.20*	Index		None
Lifepath 2010	1.20*	segments		None
Lifepath 2020	1.20*	of global		None
Lifepath 2030	1.20*	equity &		None
Lifepath 2040	1.20*	debt		None
		markets—		
		attempts		
		to replicate		
		perfor-		
		mance		
Overland Asset Allocation A	1.30	Flexible Enhanced	Various	4.50
Overland Asset Allocation D	2.05	Flexible Various Enhanced		1.00

International Stock Index Fund Rankings

Fund	Expense Ratio	Objective	Index	Sales Load
Vanguard Index European Portfolio	0.32	Internat'l	MSCI Europe	None
Vanguard Index Pacific Portfolio	0.32	Internat'l	MSCI Pacific	None
Vanguard Total International Portfolio	0.35	Internat'l	MSCI Eur. 45% Pac. 45% Emr. 10%	1.00
One Group International Equity A	0.56	Internat'l	MSCI EAFE GDP Weighted	4.00
Vanguard Index Emerging Markets	0.60	Internat'l	MSCI Emerging	1.00

e = estimated
* = no valid comparisons with other funds because of expense structure

Fund	Expense Ratio	Objective	Index	Sales Load
BT Adv. EAFE Equity Index	0.65	Internat'l	MSCI EAFE	0.50
Benham Global	0.75	Internat'l National Resources	Energy Comp DJ World Stock Index	None
Schwab International Index	0.90	Internat'l	Schwab International Index	0.75
One Group International Equity B	1.31	Internat'l	MSCI EAFE GDP Weighted	5.00
STI International Equity Index Flexible	1.45	Internat'l	MSCI EAFE	2.00
STI International Equity Index Investment	1.45	Internat'l	MSCI EAFE	3.75

International Stock Single-Country Index Fund Rankings

World Equity Benchmark Shrs. (WEBS)	0.80e	Single Country	MSCI country indexes	Neg.

Australia	Hong Kong	Singapore
Austria	Italy	Spain
Belgium	Japan	Sweden
Canada	Malaysia	Switzerland
France	Mexico	United Kingdom
Germany	Netherlands	

CountryBaskets (CB)	0.84e	Single Country	Financial Times S&P Country	Neg.

e = estimated
* = no valid comparisons with other funds because of expense structure

Fund	Expense Ratio	Objective	Index	Sales Load
Australia	Italy			
France	Japan			
Germany	South Africa			
Hong Kong	United Kingdom			
	United States			
Wright Equifunds				
WE Mexico	1.38	Internat'l	All Securities Mexico	1.50
WE Hong Kong	1.41	Internat'l	All Securities Hong Kong	1.50
WE Britain	1.50	Internat'l	All Securities Britain	1.50
WE Germany	1.55	Internat'l	All Securities Germany	1.50
WE Belgium/ Luxembourg	1.62	Internat'l	All Securities Belgium/ Luxembourg	1.50
WE Nordic	1.78	Internat'l	All Securities Finland, Denmark, Norway, Sweden	1.50
WE Japan	1.83	Internat'l	All Securities Japan	1.50
WE Netherlands	1.93	Internat'l	All Securities Netherlands	1.50
WE Switzerland	2.00	Internat'l	All Securities Switzerland	1.50

e = estimated
* = no valid comparisons with other funds because of expense structure

8

Doing the Paperwork

A verbal contract isn't worth the paper it's written on.

Samuel Goldwyn

Deciding how you want to invest and with whom entails two broad choices: with mutual funds directly or one- (or two-) stop shopping with discount brokers.

* If you invest directly with a fund family, you can usually get an all-inclusive quarterly statement including all your funds. This is the lowest-cost route, but also the one that might require the most paperwork, depending on how many mutual fund families you choose.
* One-stop shopping—where you may or may not pay transaction fees through discount brokers—is a bit more expensive, but many feel it is worth the convenience. Many no-load funds are now offered through discount brokers without transaction fees, but most have boosted their annual expenses to offset the supposed free lunch. There is one nice feature: If you invest in bonds or stocks, they can also be held in the same account with your funds.

The trade-off is cost versus convenience. If you are going to be making only occasional transactions and want the lowest costs, you are better off investing directly with the funds. If you are likely to make changes frequently, want to receive a monthly rather than a quarterly statement, and are willing to pay for convenience, a discount broker is probably a better choice.

The following is a list of discount brokers who offer a reasonably large selection of no-load funds, including index funds. Fees vary widely. We have had personal experience with only Charles Schwab and Jack White and have been pleased with the quality of services from both.

Brokerage Firm	800 Telephone #
Accutrade	228-3011
Fidelity Brokerage Services	544-8666
Charles Schwab & Co.	435-4000
Muriel Siebert	872-0444
Waterhouse Securities	934-3411
Jack White & Co.	233-3411

Index Fund Directory

Too much of a good thing can be wonderful.

Mae West

After all the cerebral work has been done, the only tasks left are completing the paperwork and sending it in along with your check. The following directory enables you to compare index funds by their objectives, target indexes, loads, and expense ratios. It also provides an 800 number for contacting them.

Fund	800 #	Obj.	Index	Max. Load	Expense Ratio
ASM	445-2763	GI	Dow Jones 30	None	0.75
Atlanta Growth	899-4742	SE	Atlanta Companies	3.75	6.49
Benham Global Natl. Resources	331-8331	NR	Energy Comp. Dow J World Stk. Idx.	None	0.75
Bhirud Mid-Cap	424-2295	MC	S&P 400 Enhanced	5.75	2.68
BT Adv. EAFE	730-1313	IF	MSCI EAFE	0.50	0.65
BT Pyramid: Inv. Equity 500	730-1313	SP	S&P 500	None	0.25*
Calif. Trust II S&P 500	225-8778	SP	S&P 500	None	0.20
Calif. Trust II	225-8778	MC	S&P 400	None	0.40
Colonial Small Stock A	426-3750	SG	Smallest 1/5 Cap. NYSE	5.75	1.45
Colonial Small Stock B	426-3750	SG	Smallest 1/5 Cap. NYSE	5.00	2.20
Compass Cap Index Equity Port A	388-8734	SP	S&P 500	3.00	0.65
Compass Cap Index Equity Port B	388-8734	SP	S&P 500	4.50	1.40

*No valid comparison with other funds because of expense structure.
Check current sales charges, expense ratios, and fees—*some funds indicated revised fees and loads were under consideration.*

Fund	800 #	Obj.	Index	Max. Load	Expense Ratio
Country Baskets (Listed NYSE)	(888) 822-4636	IF	Financial Times/S&P Country Indexes	Neg. Neg.	0.84e 0.84e
Australia	822-4636		Australia	Neg.	0.84e
France	822-4636		France	Neg.	0.84e
Germany	822-4636		Germany	Neg.	0.84e
Hong Kong	822-4636		Hong Kong	Neg.	0.84e
Italy	822-4636		Italy	Neg.	0.84e
Japan	822-4636		Japan	Neg.	0.84e
South Africa	822-4636		South Africa	Neg.	0.84e
United Kingdom	822-4636		United Kingdom	Neg.	0.84e
United States	822-4636		United States	Neg.	0.84e
Dean Witter Value Added Mkt. Equity	869-3863	GI	S&P 500 Enhanced	5.00	1.64
Domini Social Equity	762-6814	G	400 Co. Index Social Criteria	None	0.90*
Dreyfus Institutional S&P 500	782-6620	SP	S&P 500	None	0.20
Dreyfus Bond Market Index	782-6620	FI	Lehman Govt./ Corp. Bond Index	None	0.65
Drefus Mid-Cap	782-6620	G	S&P 400	None	0.50
Dreyfus S&P 500	782-6620	GI	S&P 500	None	0.55

*No valid comparison with other funds because of expense structure.
Check current sales charges, expense ratios, and fees—*some funds indicated revised fees and loads were under consideration.*

Fund	800 #	Obj.	Index	Max. Load	Expense Ratio
Federated Bond Index	245-4770	FI	Lehman Aggregate Bond Index	None	0.29
Federated Max-Cap	245-4770	SP	S&P 500	None	0.29
Federated Mid-Cap	245-4770	MC	S&P 400	None	0.60
Federated Mini-Cap	245-4770	SG	Russell 2000	None	0.73
Fidelity Market Index	544-8888	SP	S&P 500	None	0.45
Fidelity U.S. Bond Index	544-8888	FI	Lehman Aggregate Bond Index	None	0.32
First American Equity Index A	637-2548	SP	S&P 500	4.50	0.57
First American Equity Index B	637-2548	SP	S&P 500	5.00	1.35
Galaxy II Large Co. Index	628-0414	SP	S&P 500	None	0.38
Galaxy II Small Co. Index	628-0414	SC	Russell 2000	None	0.40
Galaxy II Treasury Index	628-0414	FI	Salomon Investment Grade Bond Index	None	0.40

*No valid comparison with other funds because of expense structure.
Check current sales charges, expense ratios, and fees—*some funds indicated revised fees and loads were under consideration.*

Fund	800 #	Obj.	Index	Max. Load	Expense Ratio
Galaxy II Utility Index	628-0414	UT	Russell 1000 Utility Subset	None	0.40
Gateway Index Plus	354-6339	GI	S&P 100 Enhanced	None	1.21
Gateway Small-Cap Index	354-6339	SG	Wilshire Small-Cap Index (90%)	None	2.00
Goldman Sachs Core F/I Instl.	N/A	FI	N/A	N/A	N/A
Harris Insight Index Fund Cl. A	982-8782	GI	S&P 500	4.50	0.70
Harris Insight Index Fund Cl. C	982-8782	GI	S&P 500	None	0.45
Jackson Natl. Growth	888-3863	SP	S&P 500	4.75	0.46
Kent Funds Index Equity	633-5368	SP	S&P 500	4.00	0.60
Mainstay Equity Index	522-4202	SP	S&P 500	3.00	0.90
MasterWorks Funds		FX	Index segments 17 global equity & debt markets		
LifePath 2000	776-0179			None	0.95
LifePath 2010	776-0179			None	0.95
LifePath 2020	776-0179			None	0.95
LifePath 2030	776-0179			None	0.95
LifePath 2040	776-0179			None	0.95

*No valid comparison with other funds because of expense structure.

Check current sales charges, expense ratios, and fees—*some funds indicated revised fees and loads were under consideration.*

Fund	800 #	Obj.	Index	Max. Load	Expense Ratio
MasterWorks S&P Stock Fund	776-0179	GI	S&P 500	None	0.20
Munder Index 500 A	239-3334	SP	S&P 500	2.50	0.35
Munder Index 500 B	239-3334	SP	S&P 500	None	0.70
Overland Asset Allocation D	552-9612	FX	Flexible Enhanced	1.00	2.05
Nations Equity Index Trust A	321-7854	SP	S&P 500	None	0.35
Norwest Advantage Index Fund	338-1348	SP	S&P 500	None	0.50
One Group Equity Index A	338-4345	SP	S&P 500	4.50	0.56
One Group Equity Index B	338-4345	SP	S&P 500	5.00	1.31
One Group Intl. Equity A	338-4345	IF	MSCI EAFE GDP Weighted	4.50	0.56
One Group Intl. Equity B	338-4345	IF	MSCI EAFE GDP Weighted	5.00	1.31
Overland Asset Allocation A	552-9612	FX	Various— Asset Allocation	4.50	1.30

*No valid comparison with other funds because of expense structure.
Check current sales charges, expense ratios, and fees—*some funds indicated revised fees and loads were under consideration.*

Fund	800 #	Obj.	Index	Max. Load	Expense Ratio
Principal Pres. PSE Tech. Index	826-4600	S	Pac. Stk. Exch. Tech. Index	4.50	0.80
Portico Bond IMMEDX	982-8909	FI	Lehman Intl. Govt./Corp. Bond Index	2.00	0.70
Portico Equity Index	982-8909	SP	S&P 500	4.00	0.72
Portico Interm. Bond Market	982-8909	FI	Lehman Intl. Govt./Corp. Bond Index	2.00	0.75
Portico Short Bond Market	982-8909	FI	Lehman 1–3 Yr. Term Govt./Corp. Bond Index	2.00	0.75
T. Rowe Price Index: Equity	638-5660	SP	S&P 500	None	0.45
Principal Pres. S&P 100	826-4600	GI	S&P 100 Enhanced	4.50	1.20
Rushmore Amer. Gas Index	621-7874	NR	Amer. Gas Assoc. Stock Index	None	0.85
S&P Mid-Cap (Listed ASE)	THE-AMEX	G	S&P 400	Neg.	0.30
SPDR 500 (Listed ASE)	THE-AMEX	GI	S&P 500	Neg.	0.19
Schwab S&P	838-0650	GI	S&P 500	None	0.28
Schwab S&P 500 Investor Shares	838-0650	GI	S&P 500	None	0.49

*No valid comparison with other funds because of expense structure.
Check current sales charges, expense ratios, and fees—*some funds indicated revised fees and loads were under consideration.*

Fund	800 #	Obj.	Index	Max. Load	Expense Ratio
Schwab Intl. Index	838-0650	IF	Schwab Intl. Index	0.75	0.90
Schwab Small-Cap Index	838-0650	SG	Schwab Small-Cap Index	0.50	0.67
Schwab 1000	838-0650	GI	1,000 largest U.S. Corporations	0.50	0.54
SEI Index Bond	342-5734	FI	Salomon Broad Inv. Gr. Bond Index	None	0.38
SEI Index S&P 500	342-5734	SP	S&P 500	None	0.25
Seven Seas Matrix Equity	647-7327	G	S&P 500 Enhanced	None	0.68
Seven Seas S&P 500	647-7327	SP	S&P 500	None	0.19
Smith Breeden Market Tracking	221-3138	GI	S&P 500 Enhanced	None	0.90
Smith Breeden Int. Dur. U.S. Gvt.	221-3138	FI	Salomon Mortg. Idx. Enhanced	None	0.70
Smith Breeden Shrt. Dur. U.S. Gvt.	221-3138	FI	U.S. Treas. 6-mo. Enhanced	None	0.70
STI Intl. Equity Index Inv.	355-2673	IF	MSCI EAFE	3.75	1.45

*No valid comparison with other funds because of expense structure.
Check current sales charges, expense ratios, and fees—*some funds indicated revised fees and loads were under consideration.*

Fund	800 #	Obj.	Index	Max. Load	Expense Ratio
STI Intl. Equity Index Flex.	355-2673	IF	MSCI EAFE	2.00	1.45
Stagecoach Corp. Stock	222-8222	SP	S&P 500	None	0.97
Stagecoach	222-8222	FX	Index	None	1.20*
LifePath 2000	222-8222	FX	segments of	None	1.20*
LifePath 2010	222-8222	FX	global equity	None	1.20*
LifePath 2020	222-8222	FX	& debt	None	1.20*
LifePath 2030	222-8222	FX	markets—	None	1.20*
LifePath 2040	222-8222	FX	attempts to replicate performance	None	1.20*
Transamerica Premier Index	892-7587	SP	S&P 500	None	0.75
United Services All Amer. Equity	873-8637	SP	S&P 500 Enhanced	None	0.70
USAA S&P 500 Index Fund	382-8722	GI	S&P 500	None	0.18
Vanguard Balanced Index	662-7447	B	Wilshire 5000/ Salomon Inv. Gr. Bd.	None	0.20
Vanguard Intermd.- Term Bond Port.	662-7447	FI	Lehman 5–10 Yr. Govt./Corp. Bd. Index	None	0.18
Vanguard Long-Term Bond Port.	662-7447	FI	Lehman 20–25 Yr. Govt./Corp. Bd. Index	None	0.20

*No valid comparison with other funds because of expense structure.
Check current sales charges, expense ratios, and fees—*some funds indicated revised fees and loads were under consideration.*

Fund	800 #	Obj.	Index	Max. Load	Expense Ratio
Vanguard Short-Term Bond Port.	662-7447	FI	Lehman 1–3 Yr. Govt./ Corp. Bd. Index	None	0.18
Vanguard Index Emerging Mkts.	662-7447	EM	MSCI Emerging	1.00	0.60
Vanguard Index European Port.	662-7447	EU	MSCI Europe	1.00	0.32
Vanguard Index Extended Mkt.	662-7447	MC	Wilshire 4500	None	0.20
Vanguard Index 500 Port.	662-7447	SP	S&P 500	None	0.19
Vanguard Index Growth Port.	662-7447	G	S&P/ BARRA Growth Index	None	0.20
Vanguard Index Small-Cap Port.	662-7447	SG	Russell 2000	1.00	0.17
Vanguard Index Pacific Port.	662-7447	PC	MSCI Pacific	1.00	0.32
Vanguard Index Value Port.	662-7447	GI	S&P/ BARRA Value Index	None	0.20

*No valid comparison with other funds because of expense structure.
Check current sales charges, expense ratios, and fees—*some funds indicated revised fees and loads were under consideration.*

Fund	800 #	Obj.	Index	Max. Load	Expense Ratio
Vanguard Quant.	662-7447	GI	S&P 500 Enhanced	None	0.48
Vanguard REIT Index	662-7447	RE	MSCI REIT Index	1.00	0.35e
Vanguard Tax-Mgd. Balanced	662-7447	MP	Russell 1000/Mgd. Muni Bonds	2.00	0.20
Vanguard Tax-Mgd. Cap. Apprec.	662-7447	G	Russell 1000	2.00	0.20
Vanguard Tax-Mgd. Gr. & Inc.	662-7447	SP	S&P 500	2.00	0.20
Vanguard Total Intl. Portfolio	662-7447	IF	MSCI Eur. 45% Pac. 45% Emr. 10%	1.00	0.35
Vanguard Total Stock Mkt. Portfolio	662-7447	G	Wilshire 5000	None	0.20
World Equity Benchmark Series (WEBS) Listed ASE			MSCI Single Country Indexes		
Australia	THE-AMEX	IF	Australia	Neg.	0.84e
Austria	THE-AMEX	IF	Austria	Neg.	0.84e
Belgium	THE-AMEX	IF	Belgium	Neg.	0.84e
Canada	THE-AMEX	IF	Canada	Neg.	0.84e

*No valid comparison with other funds because of expense structure.
Check current sales charges, expense ratios, and fees—*some funds indicated revised fees and loads were under consideration.*

Fund	800 #	Obj.	Index	Max. Load	Expense Ratio
France	THE-AMEX	IF	France	Neg.	0.84e
Germany	THE-AMEX	IF	Germany	Neg.	0.84e
Hong Kong	THE-AMEX	IF	Hong Kong	Neg.	0.84e
Italy	THE-AMEX	IF	Italy	Neg.	0.84e
Japan	THE-AMEX	IF	Japan	Neg.	0.84e
Malaysia	THE-AMEX	IF	Malaysia	Neg.	0.84e
Mexico	THE-AMEX	IF	Mexico	Neg.	0.84e
Netherlands	THE-AMEX	IF	Netherlands	Neg.	0.84e
Singapore	THE-AMEX	IF	Singapore	Neg.	0.84e
Spain	THE-AMEX	IF	Spain	Neg.	0.84e
Sweden	THE-AMEX	IF	Sweden	Neg.	0.84e
Switzerland	THE-AMEX	IF	Switzerland	Neg.	0.84e
United Kingdom	THE-AMEX	IF	United Kingdom	Neg.	0.84e
Victory Stock Index	539-3863	GI	S&P 500	4.75	0.58
Weiss Peck & Greer Quant. Equity	223-3332	GI	S&P 500 Enhanced	None	1.14
Wilshire Target Large Co. Growth	(888) 200-6796	G	Wilsh. 5000 Lg. Co. Growth	None	0.80

*No valid comparison with other funds because of expense structure.
Check current sales charges, expense ratios, and fees—*some funds indicated revised fees and loads were under consideration.*

Fund	800 #	Obj.	Index	Max. Load	Expense Ratio
Wilshire Target Large Co. Value	(888) 200-6796	G	Wilsh. 5000 Lg. Co. Value	None	0.77
Wilshire Target Small Co. Growth	(888) 200-6796	SG	Wilsh. 5000 Sm. Co. Growth	None	0.91
Wilshire Target Sm. Co. Value	(888) 200-6796	SG	Wilsh. 5000 Sm. Co. Value	None	0.66
Woodward Equity Index	688-3350	SP	S&P 500	None	0.17
WPG Quantitative	223-3332	GI	S&P 500	None	1.14
Wright Equifunds Belgium/ Lux.	888-9471	EU	All securities in country	1.50	1.62
Wright Equifunds Britain	888-9471	IF	All securities in country	1.50	1.55
Wright Equifunds Netherlands	888-9471	IF	All securities in country	1.50	1.93
Wright Equifunds Germany	888-9471	IF	All securities in country	1.50	1.55
Wright Equifunds Hong Kong	888-9471	IF	All securities in country	1.50	1.41
Wright Equifunds Japan	888-9471	IF	All securities in country	1.50	1.83

*No valid comparison with other funds because of expense structure.
Check current sales charges, expense ratios, and fees—*some funds indicated revised fees and loads were under consideration.*

Fund	800 #	Obj.	Index	Max. Load	Expense Ratio
Wright Equifunds Mexico	888-9471	IF	All securities in country	1.50	1.38
Wright Equifunds Nordic	888-9471	IF	All securities in country	1.50	1.78
Wright Equifunds Switzerland	888-9471	IF	All securities in country	1.50	2.00

Key to Investment Objectives:

Index description—Enhanced: Most enhanced funds' objectives are to provide returns that exceed its target index. Some attempt to lower the risk profile of the fund without a commensurate reduction of returns.

TBA	To Be Announced		
B	Balanced	**MC**	Mid-Cap
EM	Emerging Markets	**MP**	Managed & Index
EU	European Region	**NR**	National Resources
FI	Fixed Income	**PC**	Pacific Region
FX	Flexible Portfolio	**S**	Specialty & Miscellaneous
G	Growth	**SG**	Small Company Growth
GI	Growth & Income	**SP**	S&P 500 Index
IF	International Fund	**UT**	Utility
JA	Japanese		

*No valid comparison with other funds because of expense structure.
Check current sales charges, expense ratios, and fees—*some funds indicated revised fees and loads were under consideration.*
Sources: Lipper Analytical Services, Inc., fund companies.

9

Final Thoughts

Knowledge is a treasure, but practice is the key to it.

Thomas Fuller

We want to provide a list of "dont's" that should serve to keep you from making the common mistakes that defeat most investors. In addition, we want to leave you with a few of the most important guidelines that will enable you to keep your eye on the steak instead of the sizzle.

* *Don't* try to outsmart the market. The billions of transactions that occur weekly enable the market to be "smarter" than almost all mortals. The odds of beating the mainstream market, where you should invest most of your money, are particularly bad. Even for those few who succeed, the payoff is very small.

* *Don't* think you have to be an investment expert. Even though you are in the game, you are not playing it. You don't have to have the skills and experience to bat over .400. All you have to know is how to keep score.

* *Don't* forget that it is mathematically impossible for most investment professionals to provide "market-plus" returns. After costs, most underperform the market.

* *Don't* assume that because you pay more, you get more. Unlike just about any other business, it's backward on Wall Street: The more you pay for services, the lower your returns are likely to be.
* *Don't* accept earnestness, good will, magnificent service, and effort from Wall Street practitioners, if they also come with subpar returns. No matter how enjoyable, the only reason for investing is return. You only have so much time and, if the market keeps beating you and your advisor, it's time to move on.
* *Don't* expect to beat the market if you "own" the market through managed funds that hold mostly market index stocks. If you want to try to beat the market, you have to be unorthodox and go afield into the nonmainstream investing. And just because you venture into the investment wilderness, there is no assurance of returning with a trophy.
* *Don't* pay too much attention to grand investment plans, no matter how thoroughly documented, that aim to go forward solely with a strategy that has "always" worked in the past. History is ornery enough to introduce just enough new variables to make sure you can't win the next war using the last war's successful battle plan.

Obeying the "don'ts" should help you avoid the hazards that derail most investors and smooth the road to success. In addition to avoiding common pitfalls, here are guidelines to keep you on track:

* *Pay the most attention to asset allocation; it is your most important investment decision.* If your allocation decisions are sound, most other investment problems solve themselves.

* *Keep risk in perspective.* Over the long term, the riskiest strategy is not to invest in common stocks.

* *Be sure that you diversify and stay that way.* Mutual funds provide the most immediate and instant diversification.

* *Keep it simple.* Investment success depends on asset allocation, diversification, and risk management, not on complexity.

* *Trust in time and forget market timing.* Allow time to work its compounding magic for you; let market timing inflict its miseries on someone else.

* *Keep score.* If your funds are providing the market returns, leave them alone. Resist the temptation to improve on things. If they aren't, the quickest way to "catch up" is to index.

* *Trust not in the experts,* but in the market itself and in your own intuition and intelligence.

Appendix A

Questions and Answers

Q. **Why index mutual funds?**

A. Because they beat the performance of most managed mutual funds.

Q. **How do index funds beat managed funds?**

A. Costs: Managed funds are burdened by 2% annual costs versus index funds' 0.2–0.3%. Two percent might not sound like much, but it is formidable when it is chopped off common stocks' historic 10% returns. Think about it another way: Every year, when the S&P 500 Index starts the 100-yard dash at the starting line, S&P Index funds start only two or three yards behind. Managed growth and income funds, however, start 20 yards behind, and history shows that most never catch up.

Q. **Why aren't stockbrokers and mutual fund companies recommending them?**

A. They don't get paid for recommending them, even though most of the funds they recommend turn out to be below-average performers.

Q. **Why do managed funds deliver below-average returns?**

A. In addition to the very important cost factor, the other reason is that above-average performance by most participants in any activity is mathematically impossible. Since managed funds start off behind the cost eight ball, very few ever catch up.

Q. **You're saying that funds with no management do better than those with experienced professional management?**

A. Absolutely. It's not just our opinion. Over 20 years of statistics prove it. The managed funds' problem is that their managers are all experienced professionals, and their collective efforts cancel each other out.

Q. **I should therefore invest a portion of my life savings in index funds with absolutely no management?**

A. Ultimately, there is plenty of management running companies you've invested in. If your index fund invests in the largest and most powerful companies in the United States, such as General Electric, Exxon, and Coca-Cola, you've got layers upon layers of corporate management working in their best interest and yours.

Q. **But how can I be comfortable with nobody looking out for my personal interests?**

A. Admittedly, after decades of Wall Street's assurance that they know best how to invest your money, the no-management idea takes some getting used to. Index fund investors have found that, once they've invested, it gets real easy real fast; like Mother Nature, Mother Market does whatever she's made up her mind to do. Talking to a professional might (or might not) make you feel better, but it really doesn't change things.

Q. **Are index funds safer than managed funds?**

A. Not a bit. If the index plummets, down goes your index fund.

Q. **That brings up a question: What do I do about risk?**

A. Asset allocation. You have to determine your own risk/reward profile and make asset allocation tradeoffs accordingly. It is not nearly as complex as many would like you to believe. Managing risk is an integral part of this book.

Q. How fast are index funds growing?

A. In less than 25 years, indexed assets have grown from zero to over $500 billion. Even though institutions have over 30% of their stock investments indexed, so far only 5% of individuals' mutual funds are. If history is any guide, indexing, like no-load funds and discount brokers, will be the next revolution to sweep Wall Street.

Q. Why haven't I heard more about index funds?

A. Most of what you hear about investing is what Wall Street wants you to hear. The ringing index fund silence stems from the fact that there is almost no way Wall Street can profit from them—compared to their other merchandise.

Q. Why can't I just pick the funds with the best records, like the ones I keep reading about?

A. Because that doesn't work. Numerous studies have shown that using superior past performance is no better than random selection.

Q. Haven't there been years when managed funds beat index funds?

A. Yes. The critical point, however, is that those years don't occur often enough compared to the years they don't. Continually working for index funds and against managed funds are the combined forces of costs and the law of averages—over the long term, a very powerful combination.

Q. Are there bond index funds?

A. There are many, and, by one important measure, they work even better than stock index funds.

**Q. Are there index funds that invest in small compa-
nies, foreign stocks or junk bonds?**

A. There are many—and many more that invest in sub-
categories such as small-cap, fast-growing companies.

Q. Should I index all my money?

A. Not necessarily. Even if index funds hadn't been created,
we would recommend that you invest most of your
money in the leading U.S. companies, such as General
Electric, Exxon, and Coca-Cola, and in investment-grade
bonds. These companies' securities trade in "efficient"
markets where indexing works best, so it is a happy
combination.

Q. What other areas should I consider?

A. High-yield (junk) bond, small-cap, and foreign stock
funds that have historically provided higher returns.
We can't make a table-pounding index case for these
asset classes because their indexing history is relatively short and the evidence is not (yet) conclusive.

**Q. So you are recommending I index my mainstream in-
vestments, and it's a toss-up whether to index my
nonmainstream money?**

A. Precisely. But remember that since we recommend
"mainstreaming" most of your investible money, most
of it will be indexed. With the rest, you may want to
use Wall Street's traditional advisor/managed fund
category. The fund-picking derbies are thriving, and
there is no dearth of folks who are more than eager to
help. We recommend some in this book.

Q. What is the bad news about index funds?

A. Besides the fact that indexing is no "fun," you will
never beat the market. (But you will beat the pants off
the average fund investor.) Also, aiming for "only" average returns is simply more than some fund investors
can bear, even though millions of them would be billions of dollars richer had they achieved "only" average returns the last two decades.

Appendix B

What You Might Already Know About Mutual Funds

Useful knowledge is a great support for intuition.

Charles B. Rogers

Obviously, to understand index funds, you should under-stand mutual funds. If you are not familiar with mutual funds, this appendix will get you up to speed. If you need a tune-up, this appendix will do that for you too. In fact, once you've digested it, you'll be surprised how easy it is to un-derstand the basic principles, and you'll know a great deal more about how mutual funds work than the vast majority of Americans—including existing mutual fund investors.

We'll make it as brief as possible, highlighting only the most important terms.

Background

The first mutual fund (then and now called investment trusts) was established in Scotland in 1873 as a vehicle for providing Scots the opportunity to invest in the fast-grow-ing United States of America. The many trusts that followed in Scotland, and later in the United States, prospered until the crash of 1929—which forced many to liquidate. This led to reforms during the 1930s—culminating in the Investment Company Act of 1940. This act provided the foundation for most of today's mutual fund industry's regulation.

What Mutual Funds Are

There are two basic types of investment accounts:

* Taxes on returns and income in the first type of account, called qualified plans, are deferred. The most common qualified plans are IRAs, Keoghs, and 401(k) plans.
* Realized returns and income in the second type of account, a **nonqualified** account, are subject to current taxation.

Every mutual fund owns an investment portfolio of securities—some combination of stocks, bonds, and cash or cash equivalents (short-term investments like commercial paper, CDs, etc.). The combination of investments depends on the fund's **investment objective,** which you will find in the prospectus.

A **portfolio manager,** who can be either an individual or a team, decides which securities to include in the portfolio in order to achieve the fund's objective.

Each **mutual fund shareholder** owns a percentage of the portfolio proportionate to the size of his or her investment. **Total assets** (all cash and securities held by the fund), divided by the total number of shares outstanding, determines the value of each share; this is called the **net asset value (NAV).** To calculate the value of their investment, shareholders multiply the number of shares owned by the NAV. All purchases and sales of a fund's shares are based on the net asset value.

The most common type of mutual fund is the **open-end fund,** in which the total number of shares outstanding varies from day-to-day. When investors buy, more shares are created and sold to them. When they sell **(redeem),** the number of shares is reduced. The number of shares outstanding is therefore "open-end."

If investors are able to purchase shares without sales commission, the fund is a **no-load fund.** If a sales charge is imposed on either the purchase or the sale, it is called a **load fund.** A sales charge that is tacked on when investors purchase shares is called a **front-end load.** One that is levied upon the sale of shares is called a **back-end** or **deferred load.** In addition, there is sometimes an ongoing distribution charge, which is deducted from the NAV annually and is called a **12b-1 fee.**

Closed-end trust (funds) are similar in structure to open-end funds—except in that the number of shares issued is fixed. Typically, shares are sold to the public once on an **initial public offering (IPO),** and the fund is then closed. Hence the term. After completion of the IPO, closed-end funds trade among investors. Shareholders can neither redeem their shares with the fund nor purchase more from the fund. Historically, closed-end funds trade in the open market at a **discount**—at a price below—NAV more often than at a **premium**—above NAV.

Finally, individual investors are known as **retail customers,** and their brokers are known as **retail brokers,** as opposed to **institutional customers** (banks, mutual funds, etc.) and the **institutional brokers** who work with them.

Mutual funds escape taxation by distributing virtually all their **income** (dividends from stocks and interest from bonds) and **realized capital gains** (profits generated by sales in the portfolio, if any after expenses) to shareholders. Shareholders are liable for taxes on fund distributions received, regardless of whether they reinvest their distributions.

Fund shareholders can profit from:

* Portfolio income received
* Realized capital gains received (more securities sold for a profit than a loss)

* **Unrealized capital gains** not received (securities held in the portfolio still held at a gain, thereby increasing NAV)

Shareholders bear all fund management and administrative **expenses.** The common measure of expenses is the **expense ratio** (a published figure), which is expressed as a percentage of total assets of the portfolio. Transaction fees, consisting of market spreads and commissions paid (a nonpublished figure that can only be estimated), are not included in the expense ratio.

Shareholders' cost consists of the combined estimated transaction fees and the expense ratio. When shareholders' cost is divided by the portfolio assets, the resulting ratio is called the **shareholders' cost ratio.**

Shareholders' **total return** is equal to:

Income
+ Realized capital gains
+ Unrealized capital gains
− Realized and unrealized capital losses
− All shareholders' costs

expressed as a percentage of the fund's NAV over a specified period of time: e.g., a 1995 total return of 31.2%. Other costs, of course, reduce the shareholder's total return: sales loads and individual custodial, administrative, and service fees. Since these vary, they cannot be uniformly computed, and are therefore not included in the fund's total return calculation.

Types of Funds

Mutual funds are usually categorized according to their investment objectives. To keep life interesting, industry gurus often have their own proprietary labels for different categories—and they don't all agree on which funds belong to which category. To top things off, more than a few funds don't invest in a manner consistent with their category (or with what they call themselves), nor do they tell their shareholders what they are.

We have to use some of the terms, but will keep them to a minimum.

* **Growth and income (mainstream) funds** invest in the stocks of the biggest and most visible companies—Exxon, General Electric, Merck, etc.
* **Small-cap funds** specialize in small capitalization companies. These are companies you probably haven't heard of—largely unknown companies that aspire to become mid-cap or large-cap companies one day.
* **Mid-cap and large-cap funds** invest in medium-sized companies, many of them recognizable. Large-cap funds are somewhat synonymous with mainstream funds.
* **Aggressive growth funds** come in all sorts of permutations, but the common denominator is taking high risks in hopes of high rewards.
* **Growth funds** are not as risky as aggressive growth, and they invest in companies that have a track record of consistent growth in revenue and earnings.

Other fund types include:

* **Sector or specialty fund** investments are in certain industries or categories such as energy, health care, electronics, etc.
* **International funds** are self-explanatory, except that some invest exclusively in companies outside the United States, and others include some U.S. companies in their portfolios.

* **Bond funds** come in every imaginable form. Some invest in U.S. government bonds, agency bonds, mortgage bonds, corporate bonds, municipal bonds, foreign government bonds; others in high-, medium-, and low-quality bonds (junk bond funds). There are different maturities in each of these categories: short-, medium-, and long-term bonds.

Finally, some funds, with different investment objectives, are grouped into **families,** which are managed and distributed by the same firm. Switching from one fund to the other within a family can often be less costly than changing to a fund outside the family.

Appendix C
Indexes and Their Definitions

Indexes provide a point of reference for evaluating professionally managed assets. In addition, by definition they are the benchmark that index funds seek to replicate or, in the case of enhanced index funds, to outperform.

Note: Not all indexes are included in this appendix—only those tracked by one or more index funds.

* **Amer. Gas Assoc. Stock Index**—American Gas Association Stock Index—tracks the returns of 106 member company natural gas producers and distributors.
* **Dow Jones 30**—Dow Jones Industrial Average—measures the returns of 30 industrial companies, leaders in their respective industries, selected by Dow Jones & Co.
* **Energy Comp. Dow J World Index** is an index of energy and basic materials sectors (excluding chemicals) of the Dow Jones World Stock Index.
* **Lehman Aggregate Bond Index**—Lehman Brothers Aggregate Bond Index—combines the Lehman Brothers Government, Corporate, Mortgage-Backed, and Asset-Backed Securities Indexes.

* **Lehman Corp. Bond Index**—Lehman Brothers Corporate Bond Index—tracks the returns of all publicly issued, fixed-rate, nonconvertible, dollar-denominated, SEC-registered, investment-grade bonds.
* **Lehman Govt. Bond Index**—Lehman Brothers Government Bond Index—tracks the returns of U.S. Treasuries, agency bonds, and one- to three-year U.S. government obligations.
* **Lehman Govt. & Corp. Bond Index** includes the Government and Corporate Bond Indexes.
* **Lehman Int. Govt. Corp. Bond Index** tracks the returns of Lehman Brothers Intermediate Government and Corporate Bond Indexes, with maturities up to ten years.
* **MSCI EAFE**—Morgan Stanley Capital International Europe, Australia, and Far East Index—a market-weighted aggregate of the 20 individual country indexes that is widely accepted as a measure for international stock investment returns. Excludes the United States and Canada.
* **MSCI Emerging**—Morgan Stanley Capital International Emerging Markets—tracks returns from 20 emerging markets: Argentina, Brazil, Chile, Columbia, Greece, India, Indonesia, Jordan, Korea, Malaysia, Mexico, Pakistan, Peru, the Philippines, Portugal, Sri Lanka, Taiwan, Thailand, Turkey, and Venezuela.
* **MSCI Europe**—Morgan Stanley Capital International Europe—measures the performance of Austria, Belgium, Denmark, Finland, France, Germany, Ireland, Italy, the Netherlands, Norway, Spain, Sweden, Switzerland, and the United Kingdom.
* **MSCI Pacific**—Morgan Stanley Capital International Pacific Index—measures stock market performance from Australia, Hong Kong, Japan, New Zealand, Singapore, and Malaysia.

* **MSCI REIT Index**—a market-weighted total return index of selected equity real estate investment trusts.
* **Russell 2000 Index** is the most commonly used benchmark for small-cap investment. It tracks the returns of the smallest 2,000 companies in the Russell 3000 Index, which measures the 3,000 companies with the largest market capitalization in the United States.
* **Salomon Broad Inv. Gr. Bond Index**—The Broad Investment-grade (BIG) Bond Index—is designed to cover the investment-grade universe of bonds issued in the United States. The BIG index includes institutionally traded U.S. Treasuries, government-sponsored (agency and supranational) mortgage, and corporate securities.
* **Salomon Mortgage Index**—Salomon Brothers Mortgage Index—represents the mortgage component of the Salomon Brothers Broad Investment-grade (BIG) Bond Index comprising 30- and 15-year GNMA, FNMA, and FHLMC pass-throughs, and FNMA and FHLMC balloon mortgages.
* **Schwab International Index**—tracks the returns of the 350 largest companies outside the United States and Japan.
* **Schwab Small-Cap Index**—tracks the returns of the second 1,000 largest U.S. companies meeting certain criteria.
* **Schwab 1000 Index**—tracks the returns of the 1,000 largest publicly traded companies in the United States.
* **S&P/BARRA Growth Index**—tracks the returns of the most expensive half of the S&P 500 index, as measured by price/book ratio.
* **S&P/BARRA Value Index**—tracks the returns of the least expensive half of the S&P 500 Index, as measured by price/book ratio.

* **S&P 100**—measures the returns of the stocks of the 100 largest companies in the S&P 500 Index.
* **S&P 400**—S&P's Mid-Cap 400 index measures the performance of the largest 400 stocks outside the S&P 100.
* **S&P 500 Index**—the most common benchmark for institutional investors measuring their returns. It tracks the return of 400 industrial, 20 transportation, 40 utility, and 40 financial companies.
* **Smallest 1/5 Cap NYSE**—smallest one-fifth of all companies listed on the New York Stock Exchange, as measured by total capitalization.
* **Wilshire 4500**—tracks the performance of 4,500 of the largest U.S. companies.
* **Wilshire 5000**—measures returns of 5,000 of the largest U.S. stocks, determined by market capitalization. Because it is one of the broadest indexes, it is considered to track the returns of all U.S. stocks.
* **Wilshire Small-Cap Index**—tracks 250 companies with a median market capitalization of approximately $450 million and reflects the general characteristics and performance profile of small companies.

Appendix D

Compound Growth (Investment Rate-of-Return Factors)

Year	3.0%	3.5%	4.0%	4.5%	5.0%	5.5%	6.0%	6.5%	7.0%	7.5%	8.0%	8.5%	9.0%	9.5%	10.0%	10.5%	11.0%	11.5%	12.0%
1	1.03	1.04	1.04	1.05	1.05	1.06	1.06	1.07	1.07	1.08	1.08	1.09	1.09	1.10	1.10	1.11	1.11	1.12	1.12
2	1.06	1.07	1.08	1.09	1.10	1.11	1.12	1.13	1.14	1.16	1.17	1.18	1.19	1.20	1.21	1.22	1.23	1.24	1.25
3	1.09	1.11	1.12	1.14	1.16	1.17	1.19	1.21	1.23	1.24	1.26	1.28	1.30	1.31	1.33	1.35	1.37	1.39	1.40
4	1.13	1.15	1.17	1.19	1.22	1.24	1.26	1.29	1.31	1.34	1.36	1.39	1.41	1.44	1.46	1.49	1.52	1.55	1.57
5	1.16	1.19	1.22	1.25	1.28	1.31	1.34	1.37	1.40	1.44	1.47	1.50	1.54	1.57	1.61	1.65	1.69	1.72	1.76
6	1.19	1.23	1.27	1.30	1.34	1.38	1.42	1.46	1.50	1.54	1.59	1.63	1.68	1.72	1.77	1.82	1.87	1.92	1.97
7	1.23	1.27	1.32	1.36	1.41	1.45	1.50	1.55	1.61	1.66	1.71	1.77	1.83	1.89	1.95	2.01	2.08	2.14	2.21
8	1.27	1.32	1.37	1.42	1.48	1.53	1.59	1.65	1.72	1.78	1.85	1.92	1.99	2.07	2.14	2.22	2.30	2.39	2.48
9	1.30	1.36	1.42	1.49	1.55	1.62	1.69	1.76	1.84	1.92	2.00	2.08	2.17	2.26	2.36	2.46	2.56	2.66	2.77
10	1.34	1.41	1.48	1.55	1.63	1.71	1.79	1.88	1.97	2.06	2.16	2.26	2.37	2.48	2.59	2.71	2.84	2.97	3.11
11	1.38	1.46	1.54	1.62	1.71	1.80	1.90	2.00	2.10	2.22	2.33	2.45	2.58	2.71	2.85	3.00	3.15	3.31	3.48
12	1.43	1.51	1.60	1.70	1.80	1.90	2.01	2.13	2.25	2.38	2.52	2.66	2.81	2.97	3.14	3.31	3.50	3.69	3.90
13	1.47	1.56	1.67	1.77	1.89	2.01	2.13	2.27	2.41	2.56	2.72	2.89	3.07	3.25	3.45	3.66	3.88	4.12	4.36
14	1.51	1.62	1.73	1.85	1.98	2.12	2.26	2.41	2.58	2.75	2.94	3.13	3.34	3.56	3.80	4.05	4.31	4.59	4.89
15	1.56	1.68	1.80	1.94	2.08	2.23	2.40	2.57	2.76	2.96	3.17	3.40	3.64	3.90	4.18	4.47	4.78	5.12	5.47
16	1.60	1.73	1.87	2.02	2.18	2.36	2.54	2.74	2.95	3.18	3.43	3.69	3.97	4.27	4.59	4.94	5.31	5.71	6.13
17	1.65	1.79	1.95	2.11	2.29	2.48	2.69	2.92	3.16	3.42	3.70	4.00	4.33	4.68	5.05	5.46	5.90	6.36	6.87

18	1.70	1.86	2.03	2.21	2.41	2.62	2.85	3.11	3.38	3.68	4.00	4.34	4.72	5.12	5.56	6.03	6.54	7.09	7.69
19	1.75	1.92	2.11	2.31	2.53	2.77	3.03	3.31	3.62	3.95	4.32	4.71	5.14	5.61	6.12	6.67	7.26	7.91	8.61
20	1.81	1.99	2.19	2.41	2.65	2.92	3.21	3.52	3.87	4.25	4.66	5.11	5.60	6.14	6.73	7.37	8.06	8.82	9.65
21	1.86	2.06	2.28	2.52	2.79	3.08	3.40	3.75	4.14	4.57	5.03	5.55	6.11	6.73	7.40	8.14	8.95	9.83	10.80
22	1.92	2.13	2.37	2.63	2.93	3.25	3.60	4.00	4.43	4.91	5.44	6.02	6.66	7.36	8.14	8.99	9.93	10.97	12.10
23	1.97	2.21	2.46	2.75	3.07	3.43	3.82	4.26	4.74	5.28	5.87	6.53	7.26	8.06	8.95	9.94	11.03	12.23	13.55
24	2.03	2.28	2.56	2.88	3.23	3.61	4.05	4.53	5.07	5.67	6.34	7.08	7.91	8.83	9.85	10.98	12.24	13.63	15.18
25	2.09	2.36	2.67	3.01	3.39	3.81	4.29	4.83	5.43	6.10	6.85	7.69	8.62	9.67	10.83	12.14	13.59	15.20	17.00
26	2.16	2.45	2.77	3.14	3.56	4.02	4.55	5.14	5.81	6.56	7.40	8.34	9.40	10.59	11.92	13.41	15.08	16.95	19.04
27	2.22	2.53	2.88	3.28	3.73	4.24	4.82	5.48	6.21	7.05	7.99	9.05	10.25	11.59	13.11	14.82	16.74	18.90	21.32
28	2.29	2.62	3.00	3.43	3.92	4.48	5.11	5.83	6.65	7.58	8.63	9.82	11.17	12.69	14.42	16.37	18.58	21.07	23.88
29	2.36	2.71	3.12	3.58	4.12	4.72	5.42	6.21	7.11	8.14	9.32	10.65	12.17	13.90	15.86	18.09	20.62	23.49	26.75
30	2.43	2.81	3.24	3.75	4.32	4.98	5.74	6.61	7.61	8.75	10.06	11.56	13.27	15.22	17.45	19.99	22.89	26.20	29.96
31	2.50	2.91	3.37	3.91	4.54	5.26	6.09	7.04	8.15	9.41	10.87	12.54	14.46	16.67	19.19	22.09	25.41	29.21	33.56
32	2.58	3.01	3.51	4.09	4.76	5.55	6.45	7.50	8.72	10.12	11.74	13.61	15.76	18.25	21.11	24.41	28.21	32.57	37.58
33	2.65	3.11	3.65	4.27	5.00	5.85	6.84	7.99	9.33	10.88	12.68	14.76	17.18	19.98	23.23	26.97	31.31	36.31	42.09
34	2.73	3.22	3.79	4.47	5.25	6.17	7.25	8.51	9.98	11.69	13.69	16.02	18.73	21.88	25.55	29.81	34.75	40.49	47.14
35	2.81	3.33	3.95	4.67	5.52	6.51	7.69	9.06	10.68	12.57	14.79	17.38	20.41	23.96	28.10	32.94	38.57	45.15	52.80

Courtesy of T. Rowe Price Associates.

Index

[Numbers in *italics* refer to illustrations.]